CICADA

ЦИКАДА

Tatiana Voltskaia was born in St Petersburg (then Leningrad) and educated at the Krupskaya Institute of Culture. She has worked as a radio journalist since 1987, and a correspondent for Radio Svobody (Radio Liberty) since 2000. Her first programmes were features on modern Russian philosophers and writers. She regularly publishes articles on cultural topics in leading Russian journals and magazines such as *Znamia, Novy mir, Oktiabr, Druzhba narodov, Neva* and *Zvezda*. She established herself as a leading poet and cultural commentator following the appearance of her first collection *Two bloods* in 1989, and published her fifth collection, *Cicada*, in 2002. She took part in the Poetry International at London's Royal Festival Hall in 2002 and in a UK tour by Russian women poets. Her poems appeared in a special Russian women's poetry issue of *Modern Poetry in Translation*.

Cicada: Selected Poetry & Prose (Bloodaxe Books, 2006) is her first book in English translation.

Emily Lygo was educated at the University of Oxford and received her D.Phil in 2005. She has also taught Russian at the University of Oxford. Her research interests are primarily Russian poetry of the post-Stalin period and translation in 20th-century Russia, and she spent several months in St Petersburg as part of her doctoral research where she interviewed many contemporary Russian poets.

TATIANA VOLTSKAIA

Cicada

SELECTED POETRY & PROSE

translated by
EMILY LYGO

with additional translations by
CATRIONA KELLY

BLOODAXE BOOKS

ISBN: 1 85224 704 5

First published 2006 by
Bloodaxe Books Ltd,
Highgreen,
Tarset,
Northumberland NE48 1RP.

www.bloodaxebooks.com
For further information about Bloodaxe titles
please visit our website or write to
the above address for a catalogue.

Bloodaxe Books Ltd acknowledges
the financial assistance of
Arts Council England, North East.

ACKNOWLEDGEMENTS
Special thanks are due to Arts Council England for providing
a translation grant for this book. Some of these translations
first appeared in *Modern Poetry in Translation*.

Cover printing by J. Thomson Colour Printers Ltd, Glasgow.

Printed in Great Britain by
Bell & Bain Limited, Glasgow, Scotland.

СОДЕРЖАНИЕ

CONTENTS

INTRODUCTION

Tatiana Voltskaia belongs to the generation of Russian poets who began to write poetry seriously during the last decade of the USSR. This generation reached maturity in the period when Russia was passing through a period of *glasnost* (transparency) and then *perestroika* (reconstruction) and were, therefore, of an age both to react to the profound and disturbing changes in their world, and to emerge as the poets of the new Russia.

Voltskaia was born in St Petersburg (then Leningrad) and has lived there all her life. She was educated at the Krupskaya Institute of Culture. After graduating she worked for a while in the library of the Institute, then at the museum of Pushkin just outside St Petersburg, and then went on to become a radio journalist in 1987. She now works for Radio Liberty in St Petersburg. Voltskaia began writing poetry at a young age and attended a poetry club for young people that was attached to a city newspaper. She maintained this interest in writing while pursuing her studies, and published her first volume of poetry *Two Bloods* in 1989. She was subsequently accepted into the Writers' Union, gaining professional status as a poet. In recent years Voltskaia's work has been recognised with two literary awards: in 1998 she received the Tepfer Pushkin Prize in Hamburg; in 2003 she won the award of the St Petersburg literary journal *Zvezda*. In 2002 Voltskaia took part in a literary tour of Great Britain; she read her poetry in London, Manchester and Oxford.

Looking back on the early, Soviet years of her career, Voltskaia remembers the trials of literary censorship that had to be endured in order to publish: how, for example, editors of journals and papers would scowl at any mention of 'the soul' – and demand its deletion from the poem. She also remembers the alternative, uncensored literature which was published in *samizdat* (self-published) manuscripts: it was in *samizdat* that she first encountered many poems which became important influences for her, but which were not approved of by the State censors. Thankfully these two streams of Russian literature have now merged into one in the post-Soviet era, and writers can publish quite freely.

Despite these improvements in conditions of publication in Russia, many Russians complain that the public has lost the great interest in poetry which prevailed during the Soviet period: in the USSR poetry was widely read and very popular, but now many people seem to prefer the detective and romance fiction that has flooded into Russia since 1991. One does not hear such complaints in the West, where we have grown used to poetry occupying only a small corner of bookshops and of the literary market, but for Russian poets and poetry lovers this development is very disappointing. Collections of poetry are now published in very small editions, and bookshops can be reluctant to put poetry books on their shelves. Arguably, however, the relationship which has endured between poet and loyal reader is more honest and more meaningful than it ever was when literature in the USSR was either controlled by the state, or, without official sanction, perceived as a protest against an oppressive regime. Now that writers have been freed from those constraining and politically charged positions which obtained in Soviet society they have been able to return to the roles that writers in Russia have long occupied – that of commentators on society and consciences of the nation. As a poet and essayist, Voltskaia has taken on these roles.

If one can draw any distinction between Voltskaia's poetry and essays it is that her poetry is a vehicle for personal expression while her essays take the form of more public discourse. The same concerns and themes appear in both aspects of her work, but while in the prose Voltskaia sets these in the context of our lives and times, and examines the implications that they have for our society, in her poetry she explores the significance which her subjects have for the individual. Thus, in her essay 'On the Ruins of Our Rome' she considers the phenomenon of love at a social level – the love which a tyrant can inspire from those under his subjugation; in the poems, however, love is almost exclusively confined to the personal and sexual relationships which exist between individuals. We find the same dicho-tomy between personal expression and public discourse even in the subject of architecture. The essay 'The Soul of Paris' (104) describes impressions from a visit to Paris, and includes reflections on Russia's relationship to Europe, and comparisons of the Gothic with the Modern and with Antiquity; in the cycle of poems 'Cathedrals' (109) we are presented with a more subjective and personal response to Gothic cathedrals.

The subjects of Voltskaia's poetry are serious; she does not entertain the flippancy of some aspects of the postmodern in poetry, for she believes that this development is only a distraction from the essential concerns which great poetry has always addressed. When I asked her what poetry should be about she replied: 'In my opinion poetry should be (if at all one can prescribe what it should be) about the simplest things in life – about love and death.' Voltskaia identifies herself with the St Petersburg tradition of poetry, whose hall of fame includes the great names of Pushkin, Blok, Akhmatova, Mandelstam and Brodsky. It is a tradition characterised by strict verse form (called 'classical' in Russian but including a wider range of metres than classical verse admitted), intellectual themes including those from classical literature and myth, and an intimate register which is suited to the salon more than to a mass audience. Of her poetic forebears, the work of Joseph Brodsky (1940-95) has had the most profound influence on her work. Voltskaia argues that she is not alone in coming under his influence – indeed, that he has become 'A Part of Speech' (the title of one of his collections) in Russia to such an extent that no modern poet writing in Russian is able to avoid an engagement with his legacy. In Voltskaia's work we find a continuation of Brodsky's preoccupation with space and time as the vectors of our lives, and echoes of his vision of Russia as a crumbling empire.

In her essay 'On the Ruins of Our Rome' (72) Voltskaia has written about the equivocal relationship that many Russians now bear to the Empire of their recent past. On the one hand, the Soviet State was inimical to many people and an object of secret (or not so secret) animosity; on the other hand, now that its power has waned and Russia has become less important in world affairs and politics, its citizens feel its absence keenly and some regret its demise. Confronting these conflicting emotions, Voltskaia explores the emotional landscape of past glory: and there are few places in the world today that embody the poignancy of an empire faded and forgotten better than St Petersburg. The peeling façades, crumbling palaces, and collapsing balconies of once grand residences have the air of ageing matriarchs quietly slipping into old age and forgetfulness. Grass and weeds grow out of derelict buildings as nature gradually reclaims ground from civilisation. St Petersburg is growing old gracefully, but slowly coming apart at the seams. No longer the setting for the pomp and circumstance of Empire, it is now the city 'where all of us shall come to dust'. In Voltskaia's elegiac, gently humorous, and very personal poetry we explore the life that persists among the ruins and debris of imperial power, the personal struggles and private concerns which have replaced the public affairs of state and tyranny.

Although Voltskaia was born and brought up in Leningrad / St Petersburg, in her poetry images of the countryside, the seasons, and the weather are interwoven with images of the cityscape. We remember Petersburg's especially damp and rainy climate in the poem 'Rain' (29), which describes a meeting of lovers out of town, probably at a wooden country house (*dacha*) of the type that many people in Russian cities possess. But places described in the poems are never purely physical. In the 'Northern Elegy' (101) summer comes late to a locus which is an admixture of the city, and the countryside, and which also carries metaphysical weight: in the course of the poem we are give to understand that this place is a representation of the Northern climate, landscape, and mentality. Places described in the poems are never purely physical; they indicate the psychological and often metaphysical position of the poet.

The snow of the long winter is omnipresent in the winter poems. Voltskaia reflects that poems which she writes in winter differ very much from those written at other times of the year: this is not surprising in a country where the contrast between the seasons is extreme, and where the extreme weather conditions affect not only everyday life, but also states of mind. In St Petersburg in winter temperatures can often drop to minus 20 degrees Celsius, and there can be as few as six hours of daylight. Although the snow is beautiful when it first falls, it soon turns grey and dirty along the roads where it is churned up with mud and stained by exhaust fumes: Voltskaia often describes snow lying in the streets as 'dead'.

In the winter poems the landscape is static: the poems describe pictures not movement. It is only when winter recedes and spring comes that the landscape becomes animated once again. During the thaw, melting snow brings the discomfort of muddy streets and puddles to St Petersburg: walking anywhere becomes an ordeal, for the conditions are those you would expect to find in a medieval village, where there are no systems of roads or walkways. It is as though natural forces overcome the appearance of civilisation that the city's palaces, avenues, wrought ironwork and elaborate bridges try to impose:

> Like a vampire, rain drinks from winter
> Through the holes it's torn in her fine white lace,
> It has eaten away at her rational Empire
> Columns, and reaches the very essence
>
> Of forgotten roads and icy ditches...
>
> ('Like a vampire...')

The intrusion of nature into the city underlines the fragility of the civilisation that St Petersburg's neo-classical facades and baroque ornament represent. Voltskaia is sensitive to the precarious balance in the city between the natural forces of the weather, rivers and canals, and the monolithic and marmoreal order imposed by the city.

No matter what subject Voltskaia addresses in her work – be it the Gothic, tyranny, the weather, or life in an empire – love emerges as the fundamental premise upon which all things in life are founded. Believing that, 'whatever subject a poet writes about, he is only ever really writing about love' (66), in her writing Voltskaia shows love to be not only the bond between lovers, but also between human beings and God, a nation and its poet, and even between an empire and its subjects. Love is what sustains existence, whether it be the existence of the 'idol' of an empire (in Voltskaia's essays, Peter the Great is identified as one such idol), or of each of us in our lives; her poetry repeats, in many variations and forms, the simple and urgent message that life is not possible without love.

In the poems that speak most directly about romantic love, motifs of shadows and reflections are central. Voltskaia uses these images as metaphors for life's dependence upon love: unable to exist without their original counterparts, these insubstantial phenomena accentuate how vulnerable we are and how dependent on others. The cycle of poems 'Shadow' (45) is written from the point of view of a female voice – the shadow – in love. The object of this shadow's love does not reciprocate her feelings, and the more she suffers his indifference, the fainter and less substantial she becomes:

> Winter has already hidden under water
> Its fragile structure of bones and veins.
> The fewer words you say to me, the more
> I grow transparent.

> ('Shadow: 7')

This absence of love denies the shadow the nurture and sustenance she needs in order to survive. Lines of communication are like the arteries of existence which supply us with the life-blood of communion with other people: once they are severed, we cannot go on living.

The ideal of love which the voices in the poems pursue represents perfection, and like other forms of perfection which we strive for in life, it is rarely achieved and can never be sustained. We find that the shadows, conversations and other images of faltering communication in these poems usually represent unsatisfactory relationships: Voltskaia's love poems are about a lack of love, or the failure of love to develop, and the disappointment which accompanies these frustrations. The different ways in which lovers fail to reach the desired union are explored in a number of poems in this collection: in many of these, time emerges as the main impediment to such a union. In her work, Voltskaia explores the way that time imposes a restraint upon love:

Here so little time's been poured
Into the green-glass bottle of space
That though somebody may be drinking,
We've tasted – when you think about it,
Precious little...

('Time')

The relationships described by the poems are always flawed because they, like all things in life, are incapable of attaining stasis – the condition necessary for perfection, but antithetical, of course, to life. In life there must be movement and variation, an ebb and flow, a strengthening and waning, and so a perfect and constant love belongs to the world of ideals and not to reality. Voltskaia uses the image of a 'pendulum of love' to represent the shifting nature of human relationships and the indissoluble link between love and time. Even in St Petersburg which, she says, has been forgotten by everyone, even if everything else has come to a stand still, love cannot escape the march of time:

When the dusk turns yellow, like a lion
In this sovereign city that none recall,
The naked pendulum of love, alone
Counts the hours.

('The Pendulum')

Voltskaia's image of a pendulum represents not only the swings from one emotional extreme to another – from the happiness to the misery of a love affair and back again – it also represents the movement of physical love: the swaying motion which recurs in the poem is identified as the movement of two bodies making love, the 'pendulum of excited flesh'. Sex is an important and significant subject in Voltskaia's poems, for moments of sexual fulfilment in the poems are the only points at which perfect love – yearned for but denied in so many poems – is realised. The boundaries that exist between people are finally broken down, and true communication is momentarily achieved before the epiphany passes, and the lovers must draw away from each other once again. We see this pattern clearly reflected in the extended metaphor of the poem 'The Incoming Tide' (51) in which a rising tide of excitement culminates in sexual fulfilment and then ebbs away again, as every tide must. This temporary fulfilment is all that one can hope for in the world we live in: satisfaction and equilibrium are the preserve of the world to come. This is one of the many moments at which we glimpse a religious belief underlying Voltskaia's work. Belief is rarely made explicit, and never baldly stated, but surfaces a sufficient number of times for us to gain some sense of its nature. Such a belief is perhaps best seen in the poet's constant searching for the sublime amid the mundane, and for hope where there seems to be none: fleeting moments of union, of understanding, and of inspiration emerge as the meaningful achievements of life in a difficult and often disappointing world.

EMILY LYGO

CICADA

ЦИКАДА

* * *

Цикаде, похожей сразу
На всадника и коня,
Никак не закончить фразу,
Летящую из огня

Полуденного – галопом,
В пустом дребезжаньи лат,
К ночным берегам холодным
Дорогой длиною в ад.

О чем ты поешь, цикада?
Об острове ледяном;
И где же твой конь? – не надо,
Я знаю, как бледен он.

Я знаю, что ты крылата,
Что падает плащ с плеча,
В глазах твоих – два агата,
В руках твоих – два меча.

Поешь о влюбленном свете
Плывущих во тьме комет.
Но песня твоя – о смерти,
И слаще той песни нет.

Cicada...

Cicada, at once resembling
A horseman and its steed,
Can never finish a sentence,
Fleeing from the heat

Of midday – at a gallop,
With the empty clang of chain mail,
To the night-time's chilly borders
On a road as long as hell.

What do you sing of, cicada?
About an island of ice;
And where is your steed – don't answer,
I know how pale he is.

I know you're winged, and that
Your cloak falls from your shoulders,
That your two eyes are agates,
That your two hands hold rapiers.

You sing of the love-struck light
Of comets traversing the night
But your song is one of death
And no other's song is as sweet.

On the Ruins of Our Rome 1 & 2

Have you ever noticed how beautiful instruments of murder are? How much care and love the human soul has lavished on them for as long as it can remember? All those elegant daggers, as silver as ripples on water, that chain mail, those stems of swords with hilts of roses in full bloom, and tender little daggers made to give a kiss right to the heart; all those swords that are narrow as pikes, and have thoughtfully cut grooves for blood to flow along, the trembling tongues of halberds, and the sharpened drops of the heads of spears and arrows – so much concentrated passion has been spent on them, so many nights spent sleepless and women neglected for the sake of faultless blades and perfect forms! The smooth and decorative hilts, the paradisiacal foliage of their carving, the scenes of battles and hunts found on long butts and barrels, the blind clusters of shot that's lovingly loaded into stocky cannons, sparkling signet rings and little flasks for poison... Even Homer never described the bearer of 'cunningly plaited braids' – not her face, nor her attire – in as much detail, or with such rapture as the famous shield of Achilles.

These appurtenances and this splendour which have surrounded death since ancient times could be compared to the adorning of the bride for a wedding, with the distinction that humankind has, all in all, devoted immeasurably more time and effort to the instruments of killing than to wedding garb: most people get married only a limited number of times, the number of times they can kill is infinite.

Perhaps the disintegration of matter is such a burning shame that death has always tried, unconsciously, to take refuge in the beauty and elegance of the objects and rituals which accompany it. It is only recently that this rule has been broken by the blunt snouts of rockets and the piggish faces of tanks, although a gloomy aesthetics of contemporary weaponry no doubt exists. But this is not the point. The point is that, as before, these objects continue to arouse in people a feeling of love.

This love has been described in literature more than once, but the most striking example of it seems to me to be the section of Pavel Vasil'ev's long poem *The Salt Rebellion* in which a Cossack caresses the hilt of his sabre:

> Like the hand of a bride,
> Amongst all that was there
> His palm found the handle
> Of his sabre.

These lines capture the very essence of the feeling that instruments of murder provoke: it is not love, nor a holy trepidation – it is voluptuousness.

Herein lies a secret which I do not pretend to uncover, but which indubitably exists: people love that which threatens them, or their loved ones, with destruction. It was not said in vain that:

Everything, everything that threatens destruction
Conceals for the mortal heart
Pleasure which is ineffable –
A token, perhaps, of immortality!

We don't know why this happens – perhaps in our souls there is always lurking the idea that this life is only one difficult episode in a long chain of existence, and that the sooner it is over, the sooner relief will come. But maybe this hidden desire for departure is no more than a diabolical seduction.

This is all conjecture. But one thing occurs to me: is the love of danger not linked to another strange phenomenon – the love of tyrants? Who, if not the bloody tyrant, draws his people out of their everyday sleepiness by giving them a nagging sense of terror, like teetering on the edge of an abyss, and an intense experience of every minute as it unfolds because it might turn out to be their last? Is it not here that the secret of power's charm lies, the charm that Ivan the Terrible and Stalin alike found in themselves, as well as many other such vampires? Is this not why leaders who have tried to change things without shedding blood have so often seemed insipid and unworthy – unworthy to such an extent that they had to be disposed of right away: torn to pieces in the public square, or blown up…

The ugliness of death hides behind the beauty of the things that serve it: uniforms, parades, monograms; rows of soldiers like leafy vegetable plots, banked up not with earth but buckshot; the enlightened emperors bending over examples of new buttonholes and aiguillettes. Pens scratch like requiems in Petersburg offices that are hidden in classical yellow-white buildings with those indispensable columns which, as astounded foreigners remark, seem more numerous than the people. The merciless snow which shields the sultry facades, the naked torsos, the laurels and acanthus bushes with fanatical stubbornness. The hanging gardens of fireworks. The courier darting into the night along a street where a carriage has just passed. The main entrance into the Empire behind which…but we won't get more specific than that. After all, everything is designed in order that we don't specify, even though nothing escapes the eyes of the bewitched… And now all this has cast off its sharp lustre. Its imperial teeth have fallen out and its claws have become blunt, the sovereign mantle has been spoiled by a clothes moth, but it still gleams in places, and sighs in the wind with its satin lining the colour of the sunset.

The confused children of a forgotten city wander through its streets, and their hearts sink at the sight of its flaking whitewash and rouge, its cracked roads and its broken windows – what could be more painful than the face of a beloved city ageing? The city that is used to concealing its blizzards with Italian pediments, and hiding the stinking, toothy grin of Imperial power with the pleasant smile of its canals and columns is, at last, paying for everything. Stripped of its sovereign aureole, it is dying and its beauty will not save it. The extensive decoration that was constructed around the state apparatus is gathering dust and going to seed; the apparatus, hidden under the floorboards, has grown hopelessly old and rusty: its mechanisms have worn out and need urgent replacement. The contents have decayed, but the precious pediment remains, for which no one now has any use. Its owners rush about in search of their daily bread, and the riches that lie at their feet are far from their thoughts. It's strange: when cut flowers have died and we throw them away, we don't throw out the crystal vase that held them as well.

Petersburg has a strange fate. Born of audacity and violence, the city surreptitiously became transformed into the spoilt, favourite child of a clumsy power; every year it gained greater purchase upon that power's heart until it finally managed to win its love. Yes, it succeeded, despite all the curses placed on it, despite the remark Kuchevsky made: that Rus only ever loved Kiev; it feared Moscow; and it didn't even acknowledge Petersburg. Perhaps Rus did not want to recognise the city, but too much power and determination met there, too many trajectories intersected at this one point. Russia not only recognised and fell in love with Petersburg, she found a new incarnation of herself therein.

And Petersburg has undergone a metamorphosis. A dead city that threatened destruction to all has revived, and got some colour back in its cheeks. It seems that its foreign seeds have given forth some unexpected shoots: the splendid blooming of architecture has choked the rattling of parades; the Corinthian crowns of the columns sway-ing before the eyes have given a little warmth to the cold of official fervour; the aquiline, imperial wings have lost their way in the tunics of caryatids. Apollo's influence has grown stronger than that of Mars. It is as if the rich carving that decorates merciless weaponry has suddenly started growing, and has become entwined with real leaves and flowers that have hidden away its predatory blade so that it has lost its primary attribute. The sovereign terror has receded and been brightened by art. Thus the dark horseman becomes a centaur, and the bloody war of Troy turns into the sunny *Iliad*.

Russia's last love came at a cost, however. It was so costly that she seemed to be waiting for an opportunity to cast this sweet ego from her. Clearly, Russia's Asiatic temperament demands the humiliation of Petersburg, and it remains for us to bend our heads to her will. Lost, we walk along the faded streets and fragile bridges, crushed by the secret of love and death which stares out at us from every corner; and the dry, mysterious wind, whipping up the dust, blows in our faces.

* * *

От горечи, струящейся в ветвях,
От ветра, отрясающего прах
С прозрачных ног, от выкриков блатных
Среди кустов в кольчугах водяных,
От времени, текущего из глаз,
От страха, покидающего нас
Лишь на минуту, на глубоком дне
Объятия, где мы мертвы вполне,
Поскольку вышли за границы тел,
От горизонта, бледного, как мел,
Песчаного шуршания газет,
Приятеля, орущего – "Привет!",
От слякоти, от пьяниц у метро
И от судьбы, что ставит на зеро,
От топота на пятом этаже,
От чайника, вскипевшего уже,
От вечера пустого впереди,
От жалких слов моих – "Не уходи!",
От сотен уст, мне выносящих суд,
Любовь – мой щит: на нем и принесут.

From bitterness that's flowing...

From bitterness that's flowing in the boughs,
From gusts of wind that shake away the dust
From wax-white legs, from shouts of criminals
Among the scrub in chain-mail shirts of water,
From time, which streams from eyes, and from the fear
That only ever leaves us for a moment in
The lowest depths of an embrace, the place
Where we completely die, or so it seems
When we have moved beyond our bodies' bounds,
And from the horizon, colourless as chalk,
And from the sandy rustle of a paper,
From a friend, who's bellowing at you 'Hallo',
From melting snow, and drunks on metro stations,
And from fate, whose odds are all or nothing,
From those footsteps pounding on the fourth floor,
From the kettle, that's already boiling dry,
From the empty evening stretching out before me,
From my pathetic words, 'Don't leave me!'
From the hundreds of mouths all judging me,
Love is my shield: on it they'll bear me home.

* * *

Сядем в кухне вечерком,
Ужин принесен.
Поболтаем за чайком
Мы о тем о сем.

И чего покрепче – лей:
Нынче вместе мы –
Станет чуточку теплей
Ужас вечной тьмы.

Самолет, как Люцифер,
Прорезает ночь.
Кроме нас на свете, верь,
Некому помочь.

Я могу заснуть одна,
Как судьба велит.
Но от этого вина
Голова болит.

In the kitchen...

In the kitchen, the end of the day,
Supper on the table.
A natter over cups of tea
The subject – nothing special.

And something stronger – pour a glass:
Now that we're together –
The spectre of eternal dark
Looks a little better.

An aeroplane is like Lucifer,
Cutting through the black,
No one, believe me, on this Earth
Is here to help but us.

So what if I must sleep alone?
That's what fate demands,
But I know for sure this wine
Makes my head ache.

ДОЖДЬ

Тихо. Даже муха уснула,
Целый час не дававшая мне покоя.
Голове, избавившейся от гула,
Весело покачиваться над рукою,
Над чертой подоконника, над садами,
Слушать: дождь копытцами не трещит ли,
Здесь ли он – серебряными стадами
Налитой трепещущий клевер щиплет…

Вот в такую ночь не хватает джинна
В той бутылке в углу – чтоб ловил любое
Приказанье.
            Что делать? Неудержимо
Одного хочу я – лежать с тобою,
Остывая медленно от пожара,
С губ пошедшего, справившись с дрожью в теле,
Снова впасть – улыбнись! – в продолженье жанра
Влажных, дикорастущих бесед в постели,
Оплетающих это простое ложе
Лучше роз – или чего там? – мирта,
Впрочем, тут цветы со всего, похоже,
Порыжелого, будто август, мира.
И от свежего терпкого Августина
К перезрелому – винною вишней – Джойсу
Я хочу блуждать, как в раю, невинно,
Наклоняя ветвь, даже если жжется.
Беспокойным движеньем касаться Пруста
И плодов, что мне достаются редко
В одиночестве, – для тебя же просто
Не бывает слишком высокой ветки.
Не боясь терновых шипов, кругами
Я хочу блуждать от Евфрата к Волге
И, внезапно сталкиваясь губами,
Обжигаться и замолкать надолго.

Rain

It's quiet, even the fly has gone to sleep
That's given me no peace this hour past,
My head, free at last from its droning hum
Sways merrily above my hand, above
The narrow windowsill, above the gardens.
It listens – does the rain have little hooves?
Is it here it comes in silver droves,
Trampling over fleshy, quivering clover...

On a night like this what is missing from
That bottle is a genie who'll obey
Any orders.
              What can you do? My whole being
Desires one single thing – to lie with you,
Cooling off gently after the fire
That's breathed from lips, and when the body's calm,
To fall once more – Smile! – to the continuing genre
Of pillow talk that's moist and growing wild,
That weaves such garlands round this simple bed
As roses never would, and nor could myrtle.
In fact, it seems that flowers from all the world –
A world that turned rust-red like August's – are here
From the fresh, astringent Augustine
To the over-ripened, sour cherry Joyce.
I want to wander, innocent as in Eden,
To pull down branches, even if they sting,
Tentatively to touch upon Proust,
And other fruits I rarely get to taste
If on my own; for you it's very easy
There is no branch too high for you to reach.
Braving the blackthorn, I want to wind
My way from the Euphrates to the Volga,
Till, suddenly, when our lips chance to meet
They burn one another, and silence takes over...

Тихо. Даже для мухи поздно,
Дождь уносится, испугавшись взгляда,
Вдаль – садами промокшими, – стадом козьим –
Устьем сердца, уступами Галаада,
Мелкими следами полна страница,
И ладонь, и щека. Все, что было, все, что
Будет, дробно выстукивают копытца,
Лишь умалчивая, где пасёшь ты.

It's quiet. Now it's late even for the fly.
The rain is fleeing, scared off by my scowl
Past sodden gardens – leaping like goats –
Beyond the heart's mouth and hills of Galaad,
The tiniest traces cover the page and a palm,
And cheek. All things past and still to come
Will be lightly tapped by tiny hooves,
That only quieten where you tend your flock.

ЛУК

Ты меня сгибаешь, как скользкий лук,
Издающий от боли предсмертный звук –
Мол, вот-вот сломается, мол, вот-вот
Упадет. Глаза заливает пот,
Тяжела рука на спине моей –
Так сжимал, наверное, Одиссей
Не жену – оружие, что верней
Пенелопы, а главное, видно, чьей
Поддается ладони. В ушах трезвон,
Хор небесный – наверное, Аполлон
Так вот целился в десятерых детей
Ниобеи – светло улыбаясь ей.
Ведь пока в открытом окне гроза
Собирается медленно – в небеса
Устремив меня, наклонив к земле,
Ты же тоже щуришься и во мне,
Озаренной вспышками, ищешь цель,
Но ее заслоняет от нас постель,
И тяжелое облако, и кусты,
Сквозь которые продираясь, ты
Учащаешь дыханье, сильнее гнешь
Полумертвый лук, унимаешь дрожь,
Наугад – сквозь вымокшую листву –
Отпускаешь – выдохнув – тетиву,
Словно душу, звенящую от вины.
И мы оба падаем, сражены.

Longbow

You make my body curve, like a longbow,
Pain extorts from it those last, dying gasps –
It says, it's going to break, says, it's going
To fall. Rivulets of sweat flood my eyes,
Your hand is weighing down upon my spine –
Thus, I guess, Odysseus once pressed
Not his wife – a weapon, that's more faithful
Than Penelope, what's more, you can see
Whose palms it yields to. Ringing in my ears,
Is a heavenly chorus – probably like this
Apollo took his aim at all the children
Of Niobe – while smiling brightly at her.
In the open window there's a storm
Slowly gathering, and you've thrust me skyward
And yourself are bowing to the earth,
Inside me, as well, you strain to see,
Lit by sparks, you're searching for the goal,
But it's hidden from us by this bed,
And the heavy rain cloud, and the scrub,
As you force your way though them, your breath
Quickens, and you press with more insistence
Upon this half-dead bow, calm the trembling,
Intuitively, forced through sopping leafage –
You let go of – with a whistling sigh – the bowstring,
Like a soul that resonates with guilt.
And the two of us fall down, defeated.

* * *

Ни в Граде, ни в миру, ни в пустыни – ни среди сумрачных огней,
Которые глазами грустными глядят из-за спины твоей,
Ни тут, на берегу заброшенном, где ржавое мерцает дно,
Скажи, ведь ничего дороже нам негромкой речи не дано –
Одно да будет мне позволено – повсюду говорить с тобой:
Где замусоленными волнами бумажными шуршит прибой,
И где серебряною утварью горит намокшая трава, –
Да будет речь твоя заутреней и всенощной, и голова
Моя, как темный улей пчелами, роится звуками в ответ –
Рыдающими ли, веселыми, сердитыми, а если нет –
Тогда душа покинет лагерь свой, растаяв, как вороний крик.
Без твоего – зачем мне ангельский и человеческий язык?

Not in the Town...

Not in the Town, nor world, nor desert, nor among the lights of dusk
Which, like eyes filled with grief, stare out from behind your back,
Not here, on this deserted shoreline, where the rusty bottom glimmers,
Say it, for in this life we're given nothing dearer than mild words. –
One thing will be allotted to me – your conversation everywhere:
Where breakers rustle like dirty, worn waves made of paper,
Where damp grasses shine as though silverware were scattered round, –
And your spoken words will serve as prime, and vespers, and my head,
Seething like a dark beehive will answer with a swarm of sounds –
Maybe they'll be the sounds of weeping, of joy, of anger, but if not –
Then my soul will abandon its abode, dissolve like a raven's screech.
Without yours – why would I need an angel's and a human's power
        of speech?

СТИХИ О ВРЕМЕНИ

Полрюмки, как всегда, не допито
И не досказано полслова:
Чего-чего – пустого опыта
Опаздывать и рокового –
Недоговаривать – с лихвою нам
С тобою на остаток жизни
Хватило б, как бывалым воинам
Бряцания – до самой тризны.

Вот только жаль, не предназначены
Для жизни здешние широты
С огромными дождями-плачами,
Замком, висящим на воротах,
Рублем, сжимаемым не скаредой,
А пьяницей в сияньи транса.
Здесь времени так мало налито
В зеленую бутыль пространства,
Что, может, кто-то пьет, а нами-то
Не много, если разобраться,

Пригублено – все больше пролито
(Поскольку чокались украдкой).
Когда мы не умрем от холода
И сырости – то от нехватки
Текущего меж пальцев времени.
Как тара гулкая, пустая,
Грохочет небосвод сиреневый,
Внезапной трещиной блистая.
Заледенев, стучу коленями,
Но там где ты целуешь, – тает.

Скажи мне слово – это самое…
Хочу смотреть не просыпаясь
Я на твое лицо, как на море,
Где мысли пролетает парус
Так близко: рябь мельчайших черточек,
Теней и бликов поединок.
Хочу, чтоб, заспешив, на корточках
Ты не завязывал ботинок

Time

Half-glasses left, as always, unfinished
And half a word left unsaid:
Some things – like vain experiments with
Being late, and fatally breaking off
Not finishing – we've done enough
To last, with interest, a lifetime,
Like clashes of armour in youth sustain
Old soldiers to their funeral pyre.

It's just a shame that life was not
Intended for these latitudes
With these vast and weeping downpours,
The padlock hanging on the gates,
And a rouble clutched not by a miser
But a drunk in the glow of a trance.
Here so little time's been poured
Into the green-glass bottle of space
That though somebody may be drinking,
We've tasted – when you think about it,

Precious little – more and more is spilt
(Because we drank our toasts in secret).
If we don't die from cold and damp –
We'll go because we failed to grasp
The time running through our hands.
Like an empty echoing container,
The lilac heavens start to rumble,
Suddenly, through the clouds they shine.
Frozen to the spot my knees are knocking,
But there, where you kiss me, it melts.

Say to me one word – you know which one…
Without waking, I want to look upon
Your face in front of me, as I'd watch the sea,
To see the sail of a thought fly past
So close: a ripple in the tiniest line,
The duel of a shadow and patches of light.
When you stop, in a hurry, on your way out,
I want you not to tie your bootlaces

В дверях, не хлопал лифтом. Корочку –
Голодному, воды – в пустыню –

Еще мгновенье, сердца сжатие,
Глоток, затяжку, звон синицы;
Растущий внутрь цветок объятия,
Не вынущий, покуда длится, –
Пои минут живыми соками,
Хоть раз о времени не помни.
Его ты делишь между столькими,
Что мне – и вечности довольно,
Где мы не пьем глотками тяжкими
Бокал, который слишком мелок, –
Лежим, пьяны, между ромашками –
Меж циферблатами без стрелок.

Nor slam the door of the lift. It's a crust–
To someone hungry, water – to a desert –

A moment more, a contraction of the heart,
A gulp, a hasty drag, a tomtit's song,
The flowering of an embrace that's growing within,
That will not wither while allowed to last, –
Feed off the vital essences of minutes,
Just, for once, don't think about the time.
You divide it up between so many
That for me eternity will suffice,
Where we won't drink with heavy gulps
From wine-glasses too shallow, –
But lie back, drunk among the daisies –
Surrounded by clocks with no hands.

ПРИЛИВ

Неслышно зарождается прилив:
Вот губы тихо трогают, как волны,
Песчаную ладонь, вот, плечи скрыв
Становятся упруги и упорны.

Вот тело всё, подобное волне,
Но не одной волне, а сразу многим,
Уже вскипает вкруг меня, во мне,
Окатывая голову и ноги,

И, то на гребне, то на дне крутя,
Уносит вглубь, как легонькую щепку, –
И шум в ушах, и я тону, хотя
За каждую волну цепляюсь крепко.

И это чудо – выйти не на мыс
Чужих миров, неведомых америк,
А, пересекши время, как Улисс,
Лечь
        возле тех же губ, на тот же берег.

The Incoming Tide

Inaudibly the incoming tide is forming:
Lips, like waves, now quietly touch
A sandy palm, now cover shoulders,
They're growing pliant and more persistent.

Now all the body is like a wave,
Not a single wave, but many at once,
And now it's seething around me and in me,
Breaking over my head and feet,

Now on a crest, and now in a trough,
Whirling, it's carried down deep, like a splinter, –
There is noise in my ears, and I'm sinking, although
I grasp on firmly to every wave.

And it's a miracle we're not washed up
On a cape in some unknown america,
Like Ulysses, we have sliced through time,
And lie down
                    by those lips, on that same shore.

МАЛЕНЬКИЕ ЭЛЕГИИ 1

Август. Цветы устали цвести.
Прогорели угли репейника. На пути
К садоводству туман простыню развесил.
Заржавели зонтики дудок, и посреди
Речки ветер бисером вышил: север.

Зелень луга сама себе, умирая, лжет.
Лист на осине, как евнух, до срока желт,
И вельвет лопуха превратился в ветошь.
Глаз, не насытясь солнцем, напрасно ждет,
Косясь на низкое небо, – нет уж,

Флейты лучей в мягких лежат чехлах,
Трубы вьюнка на глухих дворах
Потрясают воздух пронзительной тишиною.
Свет и звук на глазах превращается в пух и прах,
И лишь позднее слово цветет на твоих губах, –
Только ты не со мною.

Little Elegy 1

August. The flowers have grown weary of blooming.
The coals of the burdock have burnt to cinders. En route
To gardening the mist has hung out its linen.
Umbrellas of pipes have rusted, and down the middle
Of a stream the wind has embroidered beads: the North.

The green of the field tells lies to itself as it dies.
Like a eunuch, the leaf on the ash tree's yellowed early,
And the velvet of dock leaves has been shredded into rags.
The eye that's still not sated with sun, waits in vain,
Touching the low sky, – for it's gone already,

The flutes of its rays are lying in soft cases,
The trumpets of bindweed in lonely yards
Startle the air with their piercing silence. Light
And sound transform before you to down and dust,
And only later will the word blossom on your lips, –
Only you're not with me.

ТЕНЬ

1

Среди зданий, крошащихся, будто зубы,
Среди черного хлеба, остатков супа,
Сигарет, за квартиру и свет квитанций,
Среди желтых снегов, голубиных танцев
На карнизе под порыжелой башней,
Деревянных, зеленых и прочих башлей,
Распускающихся, несмотря на климат,
И гостей, и пола, который вымыт
В воскресенье, обеда, который позже,
Чем на час, не начнется, детей и – Боже!–
Даже внуков, фуршетов, кагора, виски,
Похорон, рождений, родных и близких
(Где их только берут!), и врачей, и нежных
Взглядов прямо в глаза – и пониже, грешных,
Среди ветра, гудящего, словно месса, –
Я есть тень, которая знает место.

2

Все очень просто: сначала те,
Кто тебя породили, извергли горячей лавой,
Застывают в глинистой темноте –
Ты для них уже долго не будешь главной.
Для остальных, естественно, никогда.
Шевелится райское древо на кухонной занавеске:
В окна дует. В ванной течет вода.
Светит чайник – хотя не греет – стеклянным блеском;
Тот, кто может, коснувшись, воскликнуть: «Будь!» –
Чтоб из мрака возникли твоя голова, колени –
Не восклицает. Облака в окне продолжают путь,
Так становишься тенью.

Shadow

1

Among crumbling buildings that look like bad teeth,
Among crusts of black bread and what's left of a meal,
Cigarettes, rent and electricity bills,
In yellowing snow, and the dances of doves
On the ledge jutting out from a faded red turret,
Among kopecks and greenbacks, and more kinds of cash
That are burgeoning here in spite of the climate,
Among guests, and here in the midst of this floor
That's washed every Sunday, at lunch which won't wait
More than an hour, among children and – God –
Among nephews and cake forks, sweet wine and whiskey,
Funerals, new babies, relations and best friends
(Where do they all come from?), doctors, soft glances
Catching my eye, lewd stares that stray lower,
In the howling wind that sounds like a Mass,
I am a shadow, who knows her place.

2

It's all very simple: to begin with, those
Who thrust you forth, like lava, into the world,
Harden and set in the clayey darkness –
You're not going to be their number one for long.
For others, of course, you'll never be so much.
On the kitchen curtain a tree from paradise stirs:
There's a breeze, and in the bathroom a tap is running.
The teapot gleams – though it's cold – with a glassy sheen;
There's one who could touch you and cry 'Come alive!'
And draw forth your head from the gloom, your knees –
He won't. The clouds keep their course across
The window, and so you turn into a shadow.

3

Чтобы существовать – мало существовать.
Надо, чтоб кто-нибудь, на ночь или вставая
Поутру, представлял тебя целиком, боясь потерять
Хоть частицу и веря, что ты живая.
Так вода сама по себе – еще не река,
А рекой ее делают берега,
Горстка звуков – еще не слово,
И уж точно не имя – пока услыхать нельзя:
Оживить его могут, произнося,
Только губы Другого.

Но Другой молчит. Может быть, потому,
Что с ним говорят другие.
Только несчастье, как снег, проницая тьму,
Открывает глаза тебе, точно Вию:
Видишь – Тени бормочущий язычок
(Кто отбросил ее – подобрать не смог, –
То ли сердце болит, то ли село солнце),
Возле Тени – торшера горячий круг,
Что очерчен движеньем дрожащих рук, –
Где она спасается. Не спасется.

4

Мимо леса, болота, заброшенных деревень,
Мимо свалки, где роется ветер в куче цветного хлама,
Бог проходит по свету, роняя тень
В виде Адама. –
Беспокойная, ступит на воду – тянет ее глубина,
Глянет в небо – и закрывает очи,
Как она беспомощна; словно изба, темна;
Тусклым окошком теплится в ней вина,
Спать не хочет.
Как она суетлива – вдевает в иголку нить,
Едет в поезде, раскрывает книгу – и все ей мало –
Быть мужчиной, женщиной, модный пиджак носить –
Чтоб забыть,
Кого она потеряла.

3

To exist – existence alone is not enough,
You need someone who will, at night, or next morning
Perceive the whole of you, who dreads that he'll lose
Even the smallest part, who believes you're alive.
Just as water alone cannot make a river,
But relies on the banks either side to give it form,
A handful of sounds do not add up to a word –
And are far from being a name – while they cannot be heard:
Only that Other's lips
Can give them life.

But the Other is silent. Maybe because
Some other people are talking to him.
Misery, piercing the dark like snow,
Alone opens your eyes, like the eyelids of Vii.[1]
You see the mumbling tongue of the Shadow
(Whoever threw it down can't now take it back –
Either his heart aches, or the sun's gone down),
By the Shadow the orb of a standard lamp glows,
It's outlined by the trembling of hands, –
She's trying to escape. There'll be no salvation.

4

Past forests and marshes, through neglected villages,
Past dumps where the wind rummages through trash,
And through the world, God's shadow falls
In Adam's likeness…
Anxious but drawn by the depths, she steps into water,
With a glance at the sky above, she closes her eyes,
So helpless! Dark, like a cottage at night, one window
Is faintly glowing, – a flicker of guilt,
She can't sleep.
How she bustles about – now threading the eye of a needle,
On the train, she reads a book, – but it's not enough –
Being a man or a woman, dressed to kill –
It's all in order to forget
Who she has lost.

---

1. Vii is a devil with huge, heavy eyelids who appears in a story of that name by Gogol.

5

Чтоб остаться неузнанной, Тень должна
Одеваться ярко, смотреть свысока – короче,
Соблюдать известные правила – не отказываться от вина,
Сигареты, и если плакать, так только ночью;
Юбку носить поуже – тогда под ней
Померещится тело; обязательно красить губы;
Так смотреться в зеркало, словно в его глубине
Она видит свое отражение, а не клубы
Мокрого снега, кривых тропинок лучи,
Желтою свечкой оплывший поселок дачный,
Не пугаться звука; не говорить «молчи»,
Не бывать на солнце – чтобы не стать прозрачной.
И не помнить, не помнить, не помнить жаркой пчелы – «люблю»,
Острого, словно стрела, душного, словно мускус;
Если вдруг повторят – замереть в углу –
И – чтоб не дрогнул уже ни единый мускул.

6

Больно, больно Тени ходить одной:
Что она ни наденет – а все босая,
Каждый лучик колет ее иглой,
Воздух голые локти кусает,
Звук царапает до крови, за версту
Слышен вздох ее – точно сохлых листьев,
И дорога жалит ее в пяту,
Если вдруг, забывшись, она помыслит
Хоть на вечер спрятаться за спиной… –
Все вокруг – дружнее смычков оркестра –
Лай собаки, музыка за стеной,
Слово, шаг, звонок – ей укажет место.
Всякий ей напомнит, кому не лень,
Что ее счастливей любой калека:
Даже тот чудак, потерявший тень, –
Лучше Тени, теряющей человека.

5

If the Shadow wants to remain undetected, she must
Dress in bright colours, look down on others – that is,
Observe those well-known rules – that we say yes to wine,
And cigarettes, and we only cry at night-time;
She has to wear a skirt that fits tight and gives
The hint of a body inside, always wear lipstick;
Look in the mirror as though from its glassy depths
Her reflection is staring back, and not just puffs
Of watery snow, of slanting paths of light,
And a cluster of dachas, yellow like guttering candles;
No starting at sudden noises, nor scolding 'Keep quiet',
No venturing into the sun that turns her transparent.
Don't think, don't think, don't think about how that bee stings –
'I love you' – sharp as an arrow, and heady as musk scent,
When, without warning, you hear it – skulk in the corner –
Stand there still, and don't move a muscle.

6

It's so painful for the Shadow to walk alone:
Whatever she wears – her feet always feel barefoot,
Every ray of light pricks like a needle,
Bare elbows are bitten by the air,
The scratch of a noise draws blood, from a mile away
You can hear her sighs – they sound like dried leaves rustling,
And the road she walks along stings at her heels,
Should she, just once, forget herself and decide
To hide behind someone's back just for one evening… –
The world will strike up in harmony, like violinists, –
A dog's barking, music from the neighbours,
A word, a footstep, a doorbell – will show her her place.
Everything that musters the effort will shows her
That even a cripple is happier than she feels:
What's more, even that freak who lost his shadow, –
Is better off than the shadow who has lost her person.

7

Зима уже скрывает под водой
Костей и жил своих состав непрочный.
Чем меньше слов ты говоришь со мной,
Тем я прозрачней.

Ты здесь еще, а я – уже почти
Растаявший, в беспамятстве зажатый
Клок облака у дерева в горсти,
Листок измятый,

Неистово швыряемый туда-
Сюда-туда, – где не найти, похоже,
Ни выхода, ни входа, ни стыда.
Ни глаз. Ни кожи.

Как ты, приоткрываются ручьи,
В их уголках – желтеющая пена,
В них мутные снега – уже ничьи –
Умрут мгновенно.

Чем реже вспоминаешь обо мне,
Чем тише ночь соскальзывает на пол,
Тем я сильней колеблюсь на стене,
Пугаясь лампы.

8

Когда я, Тень, отправлюсь в круг теней,
Цепляясь по пути за чахлый кустик,
За флаг белья, качаемый сильней,
Сильней, – и круг расступится, пропустит,

Сомкнется вновь, и за его чертой
Я потеряюсь, превращаясь в шелест, –
Не ты, я знаю, скажешь мне «Постой!
Не уходи, постой, присядь на вереск».

Я в круге том, хотя до точки сузь
Его, до восклицательного знака –
От твоего молчанья схоронюсь,
Как в круге лампы от ночного мрака.

7

Winter has already hidden under water
Its flimsy structure of bones and veins.
The fewer words you say to me, the more
I grow transparent.

You're still here, but I have almost thawed,
A shred of cloud, clasped in memories lost,
Hanging suspended in a tree's cupped hands,
A crumpled leaf

Feverishly tossed now there, now here,
Now there – where you will find, apparently,
No way out, and no way in, no shame.
No eyes. No skin.

The streams begin to open up, like you,
Foam collects and yellows in their bends where
Blurred snowflakes that now belong to no one
Die in an instant.

The more seldom you turn your thoughts to me,
And the more quietly night slips to the floor,
The more violently I quiver against the wall,
Frightened by the light.

8

When I, a Shadow, set off for the circle of shadows,
Grasping at stunted bushes along my way,
At the flag of billowing washing that's blowing
More strongly – the circle parts and lets me pass,

And closes again, beyond its boundary
I am lost, I become no more than a rustle,
And you, I know, won't say to me, 'Stay!
Don't go, but wait, sit here in the heather.'

In the circle – although you narrow it down
To a point, an exclamation mark –
I will hide myself away from your silence,
As though in a ring of lamplight, from the darkness.

Ведь даже здесь, где плачут поезда,
И где несчастья – лучшие чернила, –
Настольной лампы желтая звезда
На кухне голубой меня хранила.

И, значит, там, у талого ручья,
Где реют души будущих ромашек,
Твоя рука, а стало быть, ничья
Вдогонку мне, волнуясь, не помашет.

Не ты меня окликнешь – но зачем
Мне имя, оброненное не теми
Губами?! Запыленное совсем.
Поклажа, непосильная для Тени.

For even here, where the trains are crying,
And where misery is the greatest ink
I was saved by the yellow star
Of the table lamp in the pale blue kitchen.

And this means that by the thawed-out stream
Where the souls of future daisies hover,
This hand, which is yours and, therefore, no one's,
That pursues me in a frenzy, will not wave.

You will not be the one to hail me, so why
Do I have this name, that will not be dropped
By those lips? It's grown quite covered in dust.
It's a load too great for a Shadow to bear.

СТИХИ О СНЕ

Как заросший травой перрон – островок дневной
Мимолетной встречи. Туда же, куда душа
Ускользает во сне, – последовать за тобой
Не могу – другие спутники, кореша
Окружают ее, летящую через тьму
В край, куда засыпаешь, сквозь край, где когда-то спал.
Я прислушиваюсь к дыханию твоему,
Как татарник, выросшей среди шпал, –
К гулу поезда, к дрожи незримых дверей и скреп,
Горячо просвистевших мимо, задев едва
На пути во временный, хрупкий склеп,
Каждый раз возводимый заново. Голова,
Закатившись в ямку между твоим плечом
И ключицей, тихо колышется на ветру,
Говорящем прерывисто, но о чем –
Может быть, узнаю, когда умру.
Ибо малой смерти вспышка, в которой плоть
Растворяет плоть, образуя слепящий сплав,
Слишком быстро гаснет, чтоб ухитриться хоть
Что-нибудь разобрать, –

                ни слова не разобрав
Из небесного хора, ни шороха близких крыл,
Ни лица твоего озаренных черт,
Ни теней, что их окружают, – лежу без сил
Горсткой пепла на теплом твоем плече.
Приникаю ухом к смуглой земле твоей,
Провожаю выглядом из-под прикрытых век;
Если б даже обнял вдесятеро сильней –
Ты бессилен взять меня в свой побег:
Высока между нами стена из цветного сна,
На ее обломках, видимых даже днем,
Когда ты очнешься – выпьем еще вина
Или крепкого чаю, пахнущего огнем.
На ее камнях татарником прорасту,
Под твоим дыханьем клонясь и качаясь. Лишь
Одного мне нужно, когда перейду черту:
Ночь за ночью смотреть зачарованно, как ты спишь.

Sleep

Brief afternoon encounters are islands in time, grass
In the tracks at a country station. I can't follow you where
You've sped off in sleep; companions and travelling mates
Press round as you fly through the dark
And into the borders of sleep, past places you slept through before.
I tune my ears to your repeated breaths
Coming up like thistles between the rails,
To the roar of the train, the rattle of unseen doors,
The nuts and the bolts whistling past, without brakes,
On their path to the frail and temporary vault
That's rebuilt over and over again. Your head,
Cupped in the hollow between your shoulder
And collar-bone, trembles slightly in a passing breeze.
You're muttering away to yourself, but I'll only know
Quite what, when I'm dead, if then. The flicker
Of small-scale death when flesh dissolves into flesh,
Welded in blinding heat, is extinguished too fast
To illuminate any of this, –
                                not a word can I catch
From the heavenly choir, no rustle of beating wings,
Not even the light on your face, or the shadows nearby –
It escapes me, scattered like ash on your warm shoulder.
I press my ear to the tawny bulk of your chest,
And watch you with care from under my half-shut lids –
If I could hold you ten times more closely than this
You couldn't take me along. A wall is between us,
A wall of colourful dreams. So, on its ruins, once it's collapsed,
The remains one can see in the daytime still, we'll sit drinking
                more wine
Or that strong dark tea, smelling of bonfire and dust.
And I'll send down my thistle roots into the soil,
Bending and bobbing to the sound of your breath,
Needing one thing only as I cross the border myself:
To spend night after night pent up and watching you sleep.

[CK]

ЗЕМЛЯ

Как имени – у ветра света нет,
А вот земля – она имеет цвет,
Она черна, как черная шкатулка,
Скрывающая прочие цвета
(Так пламенную речь таят уста),
И духи в ней живут и дышат гулко.

Когда приходит, небо разломив,
Тяжелый дождь, – под ним,
                  как Суламифь,
Черна земля и каждый раз желанна:
Тонки ее зеленые шелка,
Сырого лона память глубока,
И рот цветочный – маленькая рана.

Когда-нибудь забудется, как бред,
Что было не заплачено за свет
И на одежду денег не хватало, –
Оденусь я от шеи до ступней
В изысканное кружево корней,
Фатаю обернусь – водою талой.

И дух земли с коричневым лицом
Меня украсит травяным венцом,
Молчаньем облечет, как новой плотью,
Которая просторней и нежней
Любой другой, и находиться в ней –
Как в летний вечер плыть по мелководью.

Молчание – душа и плоть земли,
Кто обрели его и соблюли,
Те счастливы, по крайней мере, живы.
Молчит песок, молчит сухой прибой
Деревьев – говорим лишь мы с тобой,
Хоть знаем, что любые речи лживы,

Earth

(from the cycle 'Four Elements')

The wind has neither name nor colour,
Whereas there's a colour to the earth.
The earth is black, and like a black casket
It hides the other colours from the world
(As lips conceal passionate words), inside
Spirits live and breathe with resonant sighs.

When heavy rains come and break the sky
Asunder, then beneath, like Shulamith,
The earth is black, and longed for every time:
Its silks of green are of the finest weave,
Its memory of a damp bosom deep
And its flowery mouth is a tiny lesion.

One day we'll have forgotten, as some nightmare,
The electricity bill we never paid,
And how the money didn't stretch to clothes, –
I will robe myself from head to toe
In precious black lace made of roots,
I'll make do with a veil – of melted snow.

And the brown-faced spirit of the earth
Will adorn me with a crown of grasses,
Will swathe me in silence, like new flesh
Which is ampler, and softer than any other,
To be inside it is like swimming
In shallow water on a summer's evening.

Silence is the soul and the flesh of the earth,
Those who sought it out and gave it nurture
Are happy or, at the very least, alive.
The sand is silent, the dry surf of trees
Is silent – only you and I are talking,
Although we know that every word's a lie,

Что слово – жало в нашу плоть; хотя
Оно – земли приемное дитя,
Но глиняную чашку человека
Оно расколет, угольком внутри
Мерцая. Говори же, говори –
До сумерек, до осени, до снега.

Пусть мы не можем вместе засыпать
И просыпаться, но за пядью пядь
Мы вместе к смерти продвигаться можем.
В каком-нибудь недальнем феврале
Сумеем мы лежать в одной земле,
Которая нам будет общим ложем.

That a word is a thorn in our flesh; although
It's a child adopted by the earth,
It cracks the clay bowl of a man
Inside which there's a tiny ember
Twinkling. Talk to me, keep talking –
Till twilight, till the autumn, till the snow.

So be it, that we can't go to sleep,
Nor wake together, but slowly, inch by inch,
We can move in tandem towards death.
Soon, in some not far off February
We'll succeed in sleeping in one ground,
And it will be a bed that we two share.

* * *

Досмотреть остаток снов,
Мне отпущенных, – и в путь.
Досказать остаток слов
Неотвязных – и уснуть.
И – идти, идти во сне
По темнеющей стерне,
И по земляной броне,
И под облаком в огне:
Словно палец по струне,
Словно рыба в глубине,
Словно холод по спине,
Словно пуля на войне.
Все равно, в какой стране
Ты не помнишь обо мне.

Snatch the remnants of the dreams...

Snatch the remnants of the dreams
That are sent to me – and go.
Say the remnants of the words
Importuning me – and doze.
And, in my dream, go forward, forward
Along the dark stubble field,
And the chain-mail of the furrows,
And beneath the cloud of fire:
Like a finger plucks a string,
Like a fish deep in the ocean,
Like a shiver along your back,
Like a bullet fired in combat.
It doesn't matter in which country
You don't turn your thoughts to me.

СВЕЧА

Живя на ощупь, за часом час
Я жду, когда изнутри,
Затеплясь, плоти твоей свеча
Тело мое озарит.

Чтоб пламя, колеблемо сквозняком,
Сквозь кожу, как сквозь стекло,
Легло на стену под потолком
И сердце мое сожгло.

Чтоб слово твое, как прозрачный воск,
Светилось. (Как больно мне!) —
Тогда я вижу весь мир насквозь,
До трещины на стене:

Клубки живучих теней в углу,
Лучи на виске твоем,
Две чашки белые на полу,
Сеть капель под фонарем,

В которую пойманы тополя,
Плоские, как лещи,
За ними, качаясь, плывут поля
На пламя твоей свечи

И черные бабочки окон, в срок
Уснувшие. Виден мне
Бредущий лесом единорог
И ангелы в вышине.

И Тот, перед Кем я на сквозняке
С тобою за часом час
Сгораю. И слышно мне вдалеке,
Как кто-то плачет о нас.

Candle

Feeling my way, hour after hour
I wait until from within
The candle of your flesh starts warming
And illumines my skin,

For the flame, flickering in a draught,
To shine through skin as glass
Onto the wall beneath the ceiling
And it burns my heart.

I wait for your word, like lucent wax
To glow. (Oh! How it's sharp!) –
I see right through the world itself
Down to a crack in the plaster:

Knotted shadows alive in the corner,
Rays of light on your temple,
Two white cups that lie on the floor,
A web of drops suspended

From a streetlight, where poplars are trapped,
They are flat-bellied, like bream,
Swaying behind them the fields swim
Toward your candle's flame

And the black butterfly windows fall
Asleep on time, I see
The unicorn wandering through the wood,
And angels high above me.

And One before Whom you and I burn
In this draft, these long hours.
And far away I hear that someone's
Crying over us.

On the Ruins of Our Rome 4

We are a people with our heads turned to look behind us; from the gloom and the spirits of the middle ages we live in, we are used to gazing into the past. The resemblances we see are striking: everything from the roaring motorcycles, horsemen in helmets (almost in armour), and the metal and leather appurtenances of musicians, to the cut of women's clothing. But the crucial thing is not what is around us or inside us, but what is on the horizon – where then there were ruins, as there are now. And all cultural movements find their conclusion if not in these ruins, then by means of them.

One vision has been haunting me recently: a fence bent double by waves and swaying like a fan, grasped by a tender and terrible bindweed with triumphant white flowers. There's a swan that's too radiant splashing around it, sorrel that's too chunky waving its rusty laminas, and a gigantic violet burdock, frozen like a winged wall. Every summer, like an eternal bride, a guelder rose mindlessly grows red. There's no child's cry, no splash of water. This is a fence which separates us from ourselves. Wherever we look, it is always before us: this fence has split time in two, and we can never jump over it nor ever find a way around it. The voice, and only the voice is empowered to overcome the insuperable, to sew up this rent where time and space have torn apart. And this is what Blok had in mind when, before his death, he foretold that in the darkness of today we would cry out the name of Pushkin to one another.

There are many names which we cry out at one another. What's more, our strange time has taken to celebrating sad and strange jubilees which died and were forgotten long ago. Imagine if people who forgot about your birthday when you were young and lonely suddenly came up to congratulate you on your 20th birthday when you'd just hit 70 – that's what these belated celebrations are like, these repeals of sentences which have already been carried out, re-admissions to the Writers' Union in hindsight. It is a dreadful carnival of the dearly departed, a demonstration of memories suddenly rediscovered. Although this is all necessary and unavoidable, all the same, the wind of today, the rain of today, can only acquire meaning and be filled with a voice that is let loose from living lips. When a poet suddenly understands the Creator's design for time and for himself he cries over his misfortune, but at the same time he embodies both himself and time, as it were, and gives them a new existence which is more real than the one that meets the eye. An epoch which does not have its own poet is, therefore, dead.

Prosody is running into difficulties towards the end of the century. The line is getting longer, the metric feet, which were shaky even at the beginning of the century, are gasping for breath now, growing heavy, and falling, at last, into the obscure sediment of prose. The light intervals of the common metres have turned into lame *dolniks*;[2] exact, pealing rhymes have given way to cracked assonance. Twisted, leaking forms now hold no meaning, one insincerity gives rise to another, and incomprehensibility masquerades as depth: Abracadabra! – euphony. The folkloric sources that seemed eternal have now dried up, the rivers of civilisation stink and give forth nothing living. Irony turns the edge of any idea on itself, and in order to overcome the resistance of a world that has run riot, the lyric must be ten times stronger than it was before.

A voice for us did exist. It was among us and in us, and we have lost it without even realising, it seems, that we lost it for our sins. This poet exists, of course; he writes and everybody has read him – at first in manuscripts, and then in books – but when Joseph Brodsky left our city my peers and I were about ten years old and that means that, for us, he never existed in the flesh. Slipping away from us he turned at once into a something like a tree of noise (a laurel?), he was transformed into pure sound, became a part of our speech (as, perhaps, he wished). As we all know, he supped from the cup of Ovid, but we suffered no less of a punishment: not to see your only poet, not to breathe the same air as him, not to tell him how you love him; the feeling of being robbed, of irrevocable disfigurement (like losing your arms or legs); and the pitiful conciliation – the weeping for his exile as once people wept for others' fateful duels.

The poet and the contemporary reader are lovers. It is largely their relationship that gives culture its shape. But whatever course these relationships run – with periods of "cooling off" and paroxysms of passion, with trials of jealousy, disappointment and betrayals – the only real tragedy is separation. That is what has happened to us: we stare across the sea from a quiet, decaying city where snow seeps into the seams, the streets are dug up, the ash of plaster work is crumbling, and there's nothing to breathe; from the Sheremetev House, which whispers opinions about who is a Russian poet and who is a Russian-language poet; from the guarded depths of Vasilievsky Island; from a winter that seems endless because we don't have our poet with us.

---

2. The *dolnik* is a metre in Russian verse which has one or two unstressed syllables between the stressed syllables in the line.

Whatever subject a poet writes about, he is only ever really writing about love. There's no such thing as a poem that's not about love. Even Baudelaire's 'A Carrion'. The expression of hatred is, after all, only a silence, only a destruction, amnesia, a black square; but any close look at a subject, any attention to detail, to the smallest and least accessible particles of the world, is an expression of love.

Among the recent collections of Brodsky's poetry which have come out, there is one which is compiled quite differently from all the others – it is made up of only the long, and longest poems. Lines are reeled off in their hundreds as though they are stretched across an invisible loom: the weft of an idea, of logic, runs across it, fastening its unravelling basis, as though the author is possessed by the idea of weaving a pattern, of filling an abyss that is yawning wide at his feet with the fabric of speech. It doesn't matter what kind of pattern we see on this fabric: flocks of birds eternally flying away, Abraham eternally leading Isaac through the desert to sacrifice, two madmen eternally relating their dreams, a soldier writing a never-ending letter to his general, John Donne eternally sleeping in his nightshirt and nightcap – what is important is that these poems, by virtue of their own immortality, talk to death, as it were, negate the fear of non-existence, the prospect of eternal separation; they fill up space with their substance, like the sea. These poems are almost the act of a theomachist, almost Jacob's skirmish with God in the night, the right to which the poet bought with his life: 'Only the size of loss / makes a dead man equal to God.' The poems grow wider, gain power like an avalanche, become filled with the fatal emptiness of space – 'To sew with one's flesh, to sew the separation'. In his *Inferno*, Dante forgot the very last circle – the circle of eternal loneliness, which turns out to be more terrible than death:

> For if we can share our life with somebody
> Then who will take a share of our death?

Consciousness, or any thought, or any feeling exists only in contiguity with things similar to oneself – like the poles of a magnet; in isolation everything becomes absurd, disappears, multiplied by emptiness, as though by nothing. God created angels and people so that he was not alone, which is to say, so that he might exist.

Space is the clothing of time; time grows out of it, wears it into holes, throws it away, and exchanges it for new space. This process fascinates Brodsky, and appears in one guise or another in almost all of his poems (he creates himself and makes us his accomplices). It is the binding hoop and moveable axis upon and within which his poems, taken all together, constitute a universe, an entire mytho-logical space with its own calendar, its systems of coordinates, and of direct, distinguishing signs and images encountered over and over again (like, for example, the comparison of a cathedral in a square with a bottle on a table). Somebody who has lost everything is left with only one option – to become everything himself. To become a country, a homeland, and love, without searching for the lost outside. This is what Brodsky achieved.

He nods to us from far off, as though from a mirror. He flickers like a Chinese shadow in the stories of his friends who have met up with him, and in the shots of a Venetian film. The proximity and attraction of his poems is inversely proportional for us to his physical remove. (And still the pain does not let up: just imagine Pushkin as an eternal exile – what threads and links, what energy fields of cul-ture would we find to be missing?) We talk and write about him in order to make contact, if not with a hand, then with paper and writing. And will we ever see him? God knows. Of course, you can't step into yourself twice, as into the proverbial river: you don't want to go to a place where there once was a sand bank, to put your foot back into a whirlpool. But all the same, perhaps, one day we will be forgiven...

СТИХИ НА ВОЗМОЖНЫЙ ПРИЕЗД БРОДСКОГО

1

Не приходи сюда. Нас нет, Орфей,
Не вызвать нас, подобно Эвридике,
Мы – только тени от строки твоей.
Снег падает. И лица наши дики.
Здесь больше нет зимы, но вечный март,
Едва земли коснувшись, тает манна,
В живых – треска, да пленная Стюарт,
Да имярек, да Римский друг. Над ванной
Залива – пар; набухли хлопья льда;
Коричневый песок похож на гречу.
И страшно мне, что ты придешь сюда –
Телесною ожившей частью речи,
Что слово, прораставшее вокруг
Прозрачным лавром – сколько ни пололи! –
Вдруг примет очертанья губ и рук
(Как Дафна, если древний ролик
Крутнуть назад); что бывшее моим
Саднящим сердцем слово – станет скоро
По улице ходить, глотая дым
(Ну чем не нос известного майора!)...
Какой уж между нами океан! –
Грудная клетка, крови переборка,
Где каждое ребро – меридиан.
Не приезжай, не приезжай, мне горько:
Теперь одежда не годится для
Того, чтоб к ней припасть губами;
Перед тобой виновная земля
Тебя не ждет и тяготится нами,
Поскольку тени в вытертых пальто
Ни встречи не достойны, ни разлуки,
И только тем знакомы небу, что
Не удержав тебя, разжали руки.

On the possibility of Joseph Brodsky's return[3]

1

Orpheus, don't come here. We don't exist.
You cannot call us like Eurydice,
We are only the shadows of your lines.
Snow is falling. And our looks are wild.
There's no more winter here, it's always March,
The manna melts on ground it's barely touched,
They're still alive – the cod, and captive Queen,
What's-his-name, and that Roman friend. There's steam
Above the bath-tub gulf; ice flakes are swollen;
And the brownish sand still looks like buckwheat grain.
I'm terrified that you will come back here
(An animate, incarnate part of speech),
That words, which rampant, see-through laurel trees
Have overgrown – though often dug for weeds! –
Will suddenly take the forms of lips and hands
(Like Daphne, if the ancient reel's rewound);
That the word which was before
My smarting heart, will any moment
Start walking down streets, breathing this filthy air
(Just like that notorious major's nose!)...[4]
What kind of ocean now exists between us! –
The ribcage, the cynosure of blood,
Where every rib is one meridian.
This is too hard for me: don't come, don't come,
Here our clothes are no longer nice enough
For you to press your lips against their cloth;
Before you stands the guilty earth, it doesn't
Wait for you, but is oppressed by us,
For shadows wearing worn-out mackintoshes
Are good for neither meetings nor goodbyes,
And are familiar to the skies only because
They couldn't hold you in, and let you free.

---

3. This poem was written before Brodsky's death in 1995. Although it became possible for Brodsky to return to Russia after 1991, he never went back to his homeland.

4. A reference to Gogol's story *The Nose* in which a major wakes up one morning to find that his nose has left his face and is gallivanting around St Petersburg.

2

Овидий, потерявший Рим,
Наверное, не выжил бы, увидев
Его растресканным, сырым
И полным варваров. Не приезжай, Овидии!
Нежнее города, цветущего в душе,
С оконными тугими лепестками,
Лепной листвой, – не вырастет уже,
А этот, как гербарий в раме,
Коснись – рассыплется в руках.
Кто сам себя в разбитых зеркалах
Увидит – призраком, – тот, по поверью,
Недолго проживет. Взлетает прах.
Как веки, слепо вывернуты двери.
Но все-таки, покуда жив поэт,
Пока возможно вымолить прощенье –
И мы живем. Овидий, Рима нет.
Сарматский мрак сквозит из каждой щели.

3

Одиссей, доверяя себя ледяному пляжу
Родины – кромке ее ржаной,
Забывает: она – не жена, но всего лишь пряжа,
Распускаемая женой.
В исчезающие под утро
Нитки улиц, узелки площадей –
Не вплестись. Прилипают влажные кудри
Волн – к вискам берегов. Одиссей,
Сам похожий на море, поющий не хуже сирены,
Быстрый, словно весло,
Вступит в город, где доходящее до колена
Время ему мало.
Лопнет асфальт, затрещат небеса на вате:
Мы любить привыкли издалека,
Непосильная тяжесть
                    живых объятий
Нас раздавит наверняка, –
Целовавших во сне, по складам разбиравших
Все слова, что ветер принес.
Странник – страшен: так долго мы ждали, на улицах наших –
Ничего не найти, даже слез!

2

Ovid, once he'd lost his native Rome,
Would probably have not survived a glimpse
Of how it cracked apart, grew damp, and how
Barbarians moved in. Ovid, don't come.
Nothing grows more tender than the city
Which flowers in the soul, with windows shaped,
Like petals taught, with leaves in stucco-work,
But this one, like dried flowers in a frame
Will crumble in your hands at just one touch.
Superstition says if you see yourself
In a broken mirror, like a ghost,
You won't live long. Ashes will fly to the skies.
Like eyelids, doors are blindly screwed up shut.
But even so, while the poet's still alive,
While we have the chance of absolution –
We, too, keep living. Ovid, there's no Rome.
Sarmatian gloom seeps out of every fissure.

3

Odysseus puts himself in the hands of his homeland's
Icy beach – its rye-coloured edge,
And forgets this is not his wife, but woollen yarn
Unravelled by his wife.
Don't get tangled up
In these threads of streets, these knots of squares
That disappear at dawn. Damp curls of waves
Stick to the cheeks of shores. Odysseus,
Is like the sea, and sings with a siren's voice,
Moves quickly like an oar,
Enters the town where time is just knee-high:
There are too few hours.
The asphalt is breaking, the padded skies start shaking,
We've got used to loving from afar,
The weight of live embraces
                            is too heavy,
Will crush us for sure, –
Who have kissed in dreams and broken into syllables
All the words the wind has brought to us.
A wayfarer is threatening: we've waited so long on our streets –
You'll find nothing there, not even tears.

The city of St Petersburg is a sad place to live. This sentence looks sad, hanging lonelily in the empty space of the page. Black letters powdered with white stand like trees in the snow. It will soon be winter.

As a rule, however, St Petersburg is an autumnal city. Eternal autumn gilds the dome of St Isaac's cathedral and tinges the wall of the Mikhailovsky castle with blood-red, and over-ripe clusters of stucco cover tired buildings with cracks. Eternal autumn embraces us with a pale sky, the yellow of government buildings, and the spiders' webs of bridges that you cannot brush away from your face.

All around St Petersburg there are forests. When their summer strongholds are shaken in the wind their borders of green are destroyed by sienna and ochre, and the towers of maples are set ablaze. The autumn forest in the rain is like ancient Rome encircled by enraged provinces: full of the superfluous luxury of light and shade, the intricately carved gold of leaves, and heavy clusters of hawthorn. A bush, edged with purple, could be a patrician leaving the banya! Sated imperial ravens waddle along through the grass occasionally crying out, and reluctantly taking to the skies.

Inside St Petersburg there are forests as well. First one building, then another suddenly becomes overgrown with thick, impenetrable forest, hoping to grow younger and to revive in its rusty shadows. First here, then there cables, braces, and nets wind themselves about columns and corners to hold back the stone body that's coming apart at the seams, to collect and stick back the leaves that are peeling away, and to put a stop if not to the blossoming summer that was originally planned, then at least to this eternal autumn.

A city without an empire is lonely. It is like a crown that has passed out of use: it is played with, and turned over in hands, has some gems and pointed ornaments broken off it, and is thrown at last into a corner and covered up with paper and office refuse.

The little fortress seems almost offended because it hasn't been a fortress for such a long time, nor a prison, and nobody is scared of it or feels sick at the sight of it; on the contrary, people find it pleasant to walk along the ridged roof between the bastions, and to drink wine, green like the sky, or red like the leaves far below.

In the fortress sits a small, lonely Peter[5] who has fixed his strained stare somewhere far off, past the cathedral, past the graveyard, past

---

5. Peter I who built the Peter and Paul Fortress. A sculpture of Peter I by the modern sculptor Shemyakin stands inside the fortress today.

my eyes and past the clock which no longer strikes. This strange sculpture by Shemyakin was installed here a long time ago. For some reason they fenced it off with silly little ropes, a toy barrier. Only now am I looking at it carefully; I've not got round to doing so before. Of course, its like a wax figure... But no, it's an uncovered, defenceless head, nervous fingers, and awkward, sharp little knees which are trying to stand more firmly. Walk around to the back and you find the empty tubes of huge sleeves, out of which spill restless hands in soft cuffs. The back of the head is thrown back. Galloons, cuffs, buttons, reproduced down to the last detail. A little armchair of doubtful style studded with pretentious nails. But all the same – take this little monster away and it would immediately feel empty here, because the statue has taken root as if it had been standing here for centuries.

I don't know how – it's unfathomable – but Shemyakin has managed to make his Peter real. Clean-shaven and puffy, with a German tailless coat on its ungainly body and frozen in a forced pose on a fragile chair in the midst of a huge country, it is as if he were cramped from all sides by the weight of his accomplishment – which is dazzling and grandiose, and quietly vanishing into the Neva's sand; surviving corners still stick up here and there. To his gaze, which has flown beyond the borders of death, this fortress seems to be made of cardboard.

Peter sits alone, like his thoughts about Europe. Stiff as a poker, he is ready – just touch him – to leap up and snap at you. His keen fingers are trembling.

The idea of an empire does not possess living and pliable flesh – in places it is empty like the bronze sleeves of Shemyakin's Peter. If you tug away the kaftan it will all fall to pieces, spiral off in different directions. In just the same way, Petersburg, which is the embodiment of this idea, is spiralling undone. And the brains of every citizen or rather, of every former subject, are aching, because they all have that well-known debris stuck in them, hidden away, rolled into their sheltered corners. You can't throw out the image of an empire as you would an old hat.

I remember demonstrations, I dredge them up from infancy. When you are four years old and sitting on your father's shoulders you aren't made sick by the beetroot soup of portraits and slogans; at that time, when the river of the crowd rose, and carried me off, swaying and becoming intoxicated, it gave me, although to no avail, an impression of magical lightness and strength. We all drank of this potion in our childhood, and to this day, albeit noiselessly, it flows in our blood.

An empire can permit itself expansive gestures. It can favour several villages simultaneously. It can exile poets to somewhere in Bessarabiya, or to the Caucasus. It can reset the course of rivers and dry up seas. None of us is, as it were, a part of this, but now, when the borders are shrinking, everybody's heart misses a beat and somewhere something grows tense, as though we've washed our clothes and they've shrunk. All of us hated the lie, hated the fingers we could feel around our throats but, despite that, it's not so easy to get out of the habit of an empire. It is as if we were so used to a certain pressure that, when we were released from it, we suddenly noticed the terrible weight of our own bodies for the first time; we saw the awkward form of the soul we always knew what to do with in the past – hide it. But what now?

Now we're ashamed. Our energy still goes into preservation. But the preservation of what? And what's it for?

All love comes to an end. Or, rather, all love comes to an end in time, for in eternity it is never-ending. The attraction of the provinces to the triumphant centre, imbued with the magic of power and strength, will one day finish as a scornful game upon a decaying sovereign. No one is afraid of him anymore. Nobody wants him anymore – not his language, not his culture, not his victories. He can slash, he can burn, but nobody even wants to remember him – not how he loved, not even what he gave – perhaps only how he punished. He proudly jerks his shoulders and walks off into the night. The thing is, that even if he loved, even if he gave, nobody forgets humiliation. When you part with somebody you have lived with for half your lifetime, you want to remember only the beatings so that you don't regret losing the kisses: caresses poisoned by humiliation are bitter and barbed like thistle. The autumn of an empire is splashed with red. The cheeks of the children glow, blushing for their fathers. The distant borders grow crimson. The black gun barrels of branches and the cold blades of twigs are bared. The clenched hand, still strong, tightens in its oblivion – to feel for, to hold on to, to squeeze, for the last time, that which is irrevocably slipping away. Blood splashes.

The shadows are waking. Drunken cries, shots – the sounds of an approaching hunt. Sated, well-groomed huntsmen pass, kicking up bitter-smelling clouds of coloured leaves. Hounds fly by, narrow as razors.

All is quiet again.

Private life is a recovery of sight; the rustle of a voice that's disturbed in the wind and flaming like an autumn leaf, soon to be severed from its native branch. Private life, the flesh and blood of time, is destroying kingdoms. It had almost disappeared, had been crossed out by the fat pencil of the state, it had receded, like a river, deep into the bloody mud, but it alone gradually washes away the unshakeable strongholds, the bronze pedestals, so that the idols that stand upon these frown and dry up. The hand, which had powerfully pointed to the distance and to new boundaries, falls; the horse, whirling forwards and upwards, shrinks to a four-legged chair; the flying kaftan sleepily folds its wings.

The wind seething in his hair flows down like sweat from a bald crown; the face that used to breathe fire freezes and twitches its icy surface; the eyes glaze over. The Bronze Horseman on the open shore has turned into a brass person held captive in his own fortress, like in a casket.

There he sits, near and not frightening – you can touch his toy-like sword, his sharp little knees – but you can't look into his eyes: he doesn't see us, but stares at some place above. His face splits into two, three, into layers, like dark water, and in the depths the bottom glimmers – the dim features of a pagan idol expecting a sacrifice.

He guards his empire as a dragon its treasure. You can hardly see him, so decked is he with the ribbons of masquerades, and showered with the confetti of medals and salutes – but the ancient wooden mouth will not calm while it is not smeared with blood. He thirsts for the oblivion of life, love and death – and for deafening "Vivats". God willing, he'll get them.

No idol can be smashed, shattered and thrown into the river: temples will sprout up again like mushrooms, even if you can't see them. An idol can only be forgotten, can only die of indifference. The private life of a tree, the private life of hands that lie on beloved shoulders, and the private life of a soul that does not notice him are all offensive to the idol. The idol of an empire, which demands adoration and blood, will live as long as hands are outstretched to him with the agreed sacrifice, but he will die of hunger if he doesn't get fed. He hopes for a gaze that's directed from the soul to the outside – he can catch a gaze like this and bewitch it with incantations of strength, valour and power. Only a gaze that is directed inwards into the soul cannot be caught; it is invulnerable and eternal.

A red leaf blows about over the head of the brass person, it falls onto his knees, past the trembling fingers. Its uneven, crinkled edges look like the edges of this country. Your soul freezes as you stare at the unmoving eyes of the idol. If you don't want to go mad, like Evgeny, turn away before it is too late.

It is quiet. It is autumn.

A raven explodes in the branches, flaps heavily away over the bastion and disappears on the other bank in the rusty forests of the palace.

* * *

В том городе, в котором мы умрем,
Собор заплесневелый растворен,
Ленивый пух витает,
Но шпилей так отточены шипы,
Как будто ждут пронзительной судьбы,
А не вороньей стаи.

Расстегнутые запонки мостов
Поблескивают, опрокинут штоф
Залива, пробка
Васильевского плавает, светла,
Но бархатом затянутая мгла
Сначала робко,

Потом смелее пробует волну
Летучим башмаком, еще одну, –
Нежна, как голубь,
Готовя нас к объятиям иным,
С насмешкой вспыхнет взглядом ледяным
Не в прорезь – в прорубь.

В том городе, в котором мы умрем,
Мы запросто привыкнем жить втроем
Со смертью, ибо,
Пустив нас во владения свои,
Она дает нам прогуляться – и
На том спасибо.

In this town...

In this town where all of us will come to dust
The outlines of a mouldered church dissolve
And lazy fluff floats by.
But the rose thorns of the spires stick in the sky
As though expecting fates who know too much
And not a flock of rooks.

The shirt studs of a bridge are pulled apart
And glitter next to the dropped silver shawl
Spread by the Gulf: what looks like foil
Off a champagne cork is Vasilievsky.
And darkness squeezed into a velvet dress
Shyly at first extends a slippered foot

To test the creeping edge of first one wave
And then another. Downy as a dove,
And intimating a still softer touch,
It stares into an aperture, an ice-hole,
And flashes mocking looks.

In this town where all of us will come to dust
We learn to enjoy the company of death,
Which chaperones us everywhere we go:
Having once got us in its power
It lets us have our fun for a few hours:
One should feel gratitude.

[CK]

МАЯТНИК

Когда желтеют сумерки, как львы
В державном городе, забытом всеми,
Лишь обнаженный маятник любви
Отсчитывает время.
Когда раскачиваются тела,
Как будто чокаются, проливаясь,
Бокалы, или два крыла
Стремительно разводит-сводит аист,
Летя на родину, – вот так под ним, рябя,
Валы сшибаются на севере и юге –
Вперед -назад, так, плача и скорбя,
Бах догоняет сам себя
В пульсирующей фуге.
Шнур телефона выдернут, окно
Завешено, и все-таки я вижу –
Прилив-отлив, ты падаешь на дно
И всякий раз выныриваешь ближе
(Достать жемчужину!); нет, то на берегу
Гнет ветер дерево в дугу
И с каждым разом наклоняет ниже,
Оно кричит, качаясь взад-вперед,
Летает маятник разгоряченной плоти
В зеленой комнате, отмеривая счет
Иной свободе,
Иному времени, стремя полет
С закрытыми глазами над обрывом
Пурпурной глины, окуная лот
Движением нетерпеливым
В раздавшиеся волны, –

                        и на треть
Не вычислить падений и сомнений,
И остается только умереть.
Вся тайна – в однообразии движений
Крыла, бокала, ветра, что пригнул
И раскачал деревья, нас обоих
В повторах нот, сливающихся в гул
На улице, рисунка на обоях
И хищной грации ленивых облаков,

The Pendulum

When the dusk turns yellow, like a lion
In this sovereign city that none recall,
The naked pendulum of love, alone
Counts the hours.
When two bodies move together, swaying,
Like glasses raised that meet to drink a toast
And chink and spill, or like the pair of wings
A stork beats up and down with steady purpose
In homeward flight; they're like the waves below,
Rippling, as they crash North and South,
Back and forth, as Bach pursues himself
Weeping and grieving
In a pulsating fugue.
The telephone is unplugged, the window has
Its curtains drawn, and all the same I see
High-tide, low-tide, you plunging to the depths,
Surfacing, from every dive, still closer
(to reach the pearl!); no, now back on the shore
The wind has blown a tree to form an arch
Which, with every gust, bends lower still,
And screeches as it's rocking back and forth,
The pendulum of excited flesh is flying
In this green room, and measuring the cost
Of another freedom,
Another time; with eyes that are shut tight
It aims its flight straight over the precipice
Of purple clay, and impatiently
It lowers the plummet,
Into parting waves –
                         and you'll miss
A third of the all the falls and doubts you're counting,
And all that now remains for us is death.
The mystery's in the single form of motion:
A wing makes, and a wine glass, and the wind
That bowed and shook the trees; and both of us,
And notes which, when repeated, merge into
The murmur of streets; the wallpaper design,
And predatory grace of lazy clouds,

Ворча, толпящихся у дома,
Блестя рядами солнечных клыков
В преддверьи грома, –
Аккорда, взрыва, рева голосов,
Удара задохнувшихся часов
О стену, ожидающую слома.

Which, grumbling and clustering around the house,
Gleam like rows of sunny fangs on the threshold
Of thunder, –
A chord, an explosion, the roar of voices,
And strokes of suffocated clocks
Against a wall condemned to demolition.

МЫШКА

К МУЗЕ

Муза, мышка моя, дунь в свечное пламя,
Мы один с тобой – ни друга, ни снега.
Новый год со старческими глазами
Умирающего в подворотне века,
Весь раздувшийся от водняки денег,
Нам не виден – пока еще не смотрели.
Вылезай, не прачься в углу за веник,
Поиграй со мной, пошурши свирелью.
Отодвинь приход пустоглазой ночи.
Вон расцвел для тебя василек горелки,
Водопад занавески бежит. – Не хочешь?
Ну, не плачь, не плачь, не дрожи так мелко,
Все пройдет. Нальется и лопнет круглый
Шар толпы за ларьками. Кульки со снедью
Отхрустят, оттеплятся телеугли
Очагов семейных. И друг приедет –
Через горы объедков, сквозь тосты, иглы
Мертвых маленьких елок, боль головную.
Неужели ты к нему так привыкла,
Потускнела шерсткой? Ведь я ревную.

Муза, мышка, не будучи человеком,
Не привязывайся к человеку, бойся
Сладких крошек в руках его; он, как в реку,
Заведет тебя в сердце своё и бросит.
Не ходи, бедняжка, бочком по краю
Века, съеденного, как сыр, до корки,
Здесь, в пустыне гиперборейской, знаю,
Уж какие песни, какие норки.
Оглянись, изгнанница, там, откуда
Ты пришла…
                    Как пламя мигает… То ли
Крест окна, в шкафу купола посуды,
То ли сосен облупленный Капитолий.
Вспомни, милая, даже здесь на святки,
Мехом вверх тулупы надев, рядились;

Little Mouse

Muse, my little mouse, come blow on the candle,
You and I are alone – no him and no snow.
New Year has the old eyes of a century
That now lies dying in a doorway,
Bloated from dropsy brought on by money,
Not in sight – though we haven't yet looked.
Come out, don't hide by the brush in the corner,
Play with me, make the reed-pipe sough.
Delay this coming of empty-eyed night.
The cornflower gas-ring has come into blossom for you,
The cascades of curtains are running – won't you come?
Oh don't cry, don't cry, stop your tiny trembling,
It'll pass. These crowds that swell up like balloons
Will burst beyond the stalls. Food bags will rustle
Away, and television embers
Will die down in family hearths. And he'll come –
Over mountains of scraps, through toasts and needles
Of small dead Christmas trees, and a headache,
Surely you're not so used to him that
You've let your fur grow dull? Then I'm jealous.

Muse, little mouse, as you're not a person
Don't get attached to a person, you mustn't trust
Sweet crumbs in his hand; he leads you easily,
To a river, to his heart, then casts you off.
Poor thing, you shouldn't go edging along
This century, gnawed, like cheese, to its rind,
In this hyperborean desert I know very well
What songs you'll find, what bolt-holes.
Exile! Glance back at the place you're from...
How the flame dances...
                              It's either the cross
Of the window and teacup cupolas in the cupboard,
Or the crumbling Capitol of decaying pine trees.
Remember, my dear, even here at Christmas,
With sheepskins inside out, we dressed up for mumming;

Что ты там нашла? Не играй в прятки,
Покажи мне, кто это, сделай милость,
К плошке с маслом и фитильком зажженным
Наклонясь, скребет тростником по свитку,
Забывая, что боги не многим женам
Разрешают выпрясть
                                    такую нитку...

What have you found? Don't play hide and seek,
Would you be so kind, and show me who
Is bending over the oil dish and lighted wick,
Is scratching across this scroll with a reed,
Forgetting the gods don't allow most wives
To spin out
            this kind of thread...

I

Горько мне писать тебе, Квинтия, горько
Видеть вместо глаз и улыбок – письма,
Лучше б мне остаться с тобою в Байях!
Я замучила нынче моих служанок:
День за днем гуляю в садах у Тибра.
Почему-то город после разлуки
Стал мне тесен, словно детское платье.
Даже Форум – будто бы постирали.
Или это душа, как вино в кувшине
С тонкой трещинкой – вытекает на пол
И принять не думает форму тела?

II

Поругай меня, Квинтия, поругай же:
Важных Пиэрид я совсем забыла,
Веришь ли – люблю проходить по рынку,
Запах рыбы, оливок и бычьей кожи,
Звон гончарного круга и струйку дыма
От медовых лепешек. Квинтия, смейся,
Что ни день я в театре, а лучше – в цирке,
Только вот на какого ни загадаю
Я возницу – никто не домчится первым,
Видно, взгляд мой с пути лошадей сбивает.
Я, наверно, больна – и богам пеняю,
Что не сделали боги меня мужчиной...
Я тогда ходила бы где хотела,
Я тотчас побежала б тогда к гетерам
Или мальчика привела б, как муж мой,
Я... да мало ли, Квинтия! Будь здорова.

I

It is galling to write to you, Cynthia, galling
To see in place of your eyes and smile – letters,
It would have been better to stay with you in Baiae!
I've driven my serving girls to distraction:
Day after day, I walk in the Tiber gardens.
Somehow, after separation, this city
Feels too small, like a dress from childhood.
Even the Forum seems like it's shrunk in the wash.
Or is it my soul, like wine in an amphora
That's slightly cracked, trickling on to the floor,
Which will not think of taking a body's form?

II

Scold me, Cynthia, scold away:
I completely forgot the important Pierides,
Can you believe I love to stroll through the market,
The smell of fish, the olives, and the cowhide,
The sound of the pottery wheel and wisp of smoke
From honey cakes. Cynthia, you will laugh
That each day I go to the theatre, or, better,
The circus, the drivers I choose
As winners, never come first –
My look knocks the horse right out of the race.
I'm probably ill, and I reproach the Gods
That they didn't create me as a man…
Then I'd have walked wherever I wished,
I'd have run at once to the Hetera,
Or taken a young boy, as my husband did,
I…well, never mind Cynthia. Keep well.

III

Ничего не скроешь от глаз подруги!
Дни идут – безумье неизлечимо:
Словно мышь голодная тащит корку, –
Чтобы жить, с опаской любовь краду я;
Мы похожи повадками. Наважденье,
Как наряд, не скинуть – вот так улитка
В винограднике пестрый таскает домик,
Не снимая его даже вместе с жизнью.
Как же быть – раз в душу мою и тело
Гость вошел со своим ключом, – конечно,
В этой тайной комнате – он хозяин…

IV

Пусть твердит глупец о любви взаимной,
Пусть ночей не спит – измеряет,
В чье из двух сердец глубже
Вонзилась стрелка.

Не смыкая глаз, пусть считает, скряга:
Друг с утра был нежен, вчера нежнее –
Задолжал на завтра. Пусть ненасытным
Глядит кредитором.

Нелюбимому – ничего не нужно!
Он раздумьем лишним не глушит чувство
И не тупит тонкую стрелку бога
О дорожный камень.

Что богатому золотые горы!
Нищему дороже подушка. Милый
Рот
        уронит имя мое – оболом:
Всех я в мире богаче!

III

There is nothing you can hide from the eyes of a girlfriend!
The days go by – and the madness is incurable:
Like a hungry mouse that drags off some peel
To survive, at great risk I am stealing love;
We are alike in our habits. We can't cast off
Delusion like a costume – we are like the snail
In the vineyard who carries his little coloured home
That he does not part with even as he parts with life.
What can I do – now that a guest has entered
My soul and body, he has his own key, – of course,
In this secret room, he is the boss…

IV

Let a fool go on about reciprocal love,
Let him not sleep at night – as he measures
Which of these two hearts the arrow has pierced
More deeply.

Eyes wide open, let him count, the miser:
He has been tender since morning, more still yesterday –
He has borrowed for tomorrow. Let him look
Like a greedy creditor.

A person who is unloved needs nothing!
He doesn't stifle feeling with excess thinking.
Doesn't blunt the fine arrow of a god
On curb stones in the road.

What good are mountains of gold to the rich?
A penny's worth more to the poor. If the sweet
Mouth
        drops my name – like an obol,[6]
I'm the richest in the world.

---

6. An ancient Greek coin that was Charon's fee for the ferry trip over the Styx
to the underworld.

V

Муза, мышка моя, что скребешься тихо?
Заждалися мы нынче с тобою друга.
Это я могу тосковать, а ты-то
Берегись, не то потеряешь голос
Эолийскую под пол свирель закатишь.
Знаешь ли, за что ты всегда мила мне? —
Что сыта бываешь и черствой крошкой:
Только он войдет, поглядит, пошутит —
И уже заблестят у тебя глазенки,
Залоснится, как будто на солнце, шерстка.
Тем и я жива. А когда он ласков,
Грусть в глазах когда он поглубже спрячет, —
Я боюсь сгореть — тяжелее счастья
Ничего не бывает, поверь, подружка.
Поздно мы заболтались. Я слышу, двери
Запирают на ночь. Письмо не вышло.

VI

Вот и еще год миновал,
      Скоро календы
Марта. В светильники всюду нальют
      Новое масло.
Новые ленты – служанкам, сластей
      Блюда – знакомым,
Новую власть подслащая, края
      Снежной одежды
Грозного бога упорно коптя
      Жертвенным дымом.
Квинтия, скоро начнутся пиры,
      И завитые
Мальчики к пестрым столам понесут
      Полные кубки,
Флейты засвищут. Все же и мне
      Радостно это:
Стану я на год ближе к черте,
      Где никакими
Больше пирами не разлучить
      Легкие тени.

V

Muse, my little mouse, why are you scratching quietly?
You and I are tired of waiting for him.
I'm the one who can get depressed – but you,
Keep yourself together, don't lose your voice,
Roll the Aeolian reed-pipe under the floorboards.
Do you know why you are so dear to me?
Because you are sated by a stale crust,
He just has to come, glance at you, make a joke,
And your little eyes are already shining,
Your fur turns glossy, as though in the sun.
That's what keeps me alive. And when he is caring,
When he hides the sadness deep in his eyes,
I am afraid of being consumed – there is nothing
More weighty than happiness, believe me, dear friend.
We've chatted away till late. I can hear the doors
Shutting up for the night. And there is no letter.

VI

And so another year has gone by, and soon will come
        the Calends of March.
Everywhere lamps are being filled
        With new oil.
New ribbons – for the servant girls, a sweet tray
        For guests,
To sweeten the incoming powers; the edges
        Of the snowy clothes
Of a thundering god stubbornly smoulder
        With sacrificial smoke.
Cynthia, soon the feasts will begin and
        Curly-haired boys
Will bring to bright-coloured tables
        Goblets full,
The flutes will strike up the music. But for me,
        What is joyful
Is that every year the time comes closer
        When no longer
Will feasts be able to separate
        The light shadows.

VII

Если спросишь, Квинтия, меня о Риме, –
Издали похож он на корабль, избегший
Ненадолго бездны. Розовеют на солнце
Холмы – парусами.

А когда волной набегают тучи,
Точно вести черные из провинций,
Кажутся дома ноздреватой пеной,
Мокрой тряпкой – мрамор,

Время свищет – вот-вот с якорей сорвемся.
Все теряют сон: кто предал, кто предан.
Тот погиб в походе, того сослали.
Сокрушаются мирты

Театральным хором. Ты не поверишь,
Но спокойна, кажется, одна только мышка,
Что живет в углу за медным кувшином,
Потому что знает:

Новый век, что придет от нашего пира,
Как пугливый раб, подбирать объедки,
Каждый кубок найдет на столе помятым
И венок – увядшим;

Только лишь вино год от года крепче,
Год от года горше любовная песня,
Только тот огонь, что бежал по жилам,
Не залить волнами.

VII

If you ask me, Cynthia, about Rome –
From afar it is like a ship that's escaped,
For a while, from the depths. In the sun its hills
Glow pink, like sails.

And when the storm clouds gather as a wave,
Like black news coming from the provinces,
The buildings appear like spongy foam,
The marble – damp cloth,

Time whistles – we're just breaking loose from anchor,
Everyone's losing sleep – one betrays, one's betrayed.
One perished on expedition another was exiled.
The myrtles are grieving

With a theatrical choir. You won't believe it,
But the little mouse, who lives in the corner by
The bronze amphora, alone appears to be calm,
Because it knows:

The new age will come to our feast
Like a frightened slave to pick at the leftovers,
Will find every goblet twisted on the table,
Every garland wilted,

And only the wine gets stronger year by year,
Year after year the love song grows more bitter,
Only that fire, which courses through the veins
Will not be extinguished by the waves.

VIII

Если спросишь, Квинтия, меня об Амуре,
Я отвечу: Амур – великий ваятель,
Он обтесывает души, как мрамор, –
Всем на обозренье.

То, по прихоти, вытешет он Хариту,
То – от горя застывшую Ниобею,
Чьи надежды умирают, как дети,
Одна за другою.

У меня под резцом его – мраморной крошкой
Брызжет разум, душа то дрожит менадой,
То смеется нимфой. Что он задумал –
До сих пор не знаю.

IX

Если спросишь, Квинтия, меня о друге,
Я отвечу то же, что ветка – о ветре,
Что о красном крае его одежды –
Пыльная площадь.

Лучше – пляшущий смоляной обломок
Корабля спроси о волне зеленой,
Крышу о дожде, чем меня о взгляде
Его печальном;

Как лицо склоняется надо мною
Узкое, оливковое, с губами
Терпкими, рука же спешит распутать
Ленту под грудью, –

Страшно говорить мне – боюсь я сглаза:
Что как срежет кто-нибудь вместо пряди
Слово, строчку вынет, как след, – сжигая
И шепча заклятья?

Что как слепит кто-нибудь, как из воска,
Из прозрачных звуков – его подобье,
Наведет болезнь? – Нет, уж лучше вовсе
Языка лишиться.

VIII

If you ask me, Cynthia, about Cupid,
I will answer: Cupid is a great sculptor,
He sculpts the soul, like marble, –
For everyone to see.

Now he carves, on a whim, the Charites,
Now – Niobe, who's frozen still from grief,
Whose hopes are dying, like her children,
One by one.

Under his chisel, like a marble chip
My reason splashes, my soul quakes like a maenad
Then laughs like a nymph. Even now I don't know
What he had planned.

IX

If you ask me, Cynthia, about him,
I will answer as a branch speaks of the wind,
As a dusty square would speak of the red edge
Of his clothes.

It's better to ask the dancing, tar-covered wreck
Of a ship to tell you about the green waves,
Or a roof about the rain, than ask me about
His sorry gaze;

As his face bends down over me,
Narrow, olive-coloured, with lips
Astringent, his hand hurrying to undo
The ribbon at my breast, –

I am frightened to speak, I fear the evil eye:
What if someone cuts not a lock of hair
But a word, eliminates a line, like a trace, burning
And whispering spells?

What if somebody models, like wax,
A likeness from transparent sounds,
Summons illness? No, it's better to completely lose
Your tongue.

XI

Квинтия, друг вчера подарил мне чашу:
Пляшут на ней серебряные сатиры.
Что мне из нее доведется выпить?
Кого из нас раньше

Ссылка ожидает – меня за неверность,
За насмешливый нрав и язык – его ли? –
Все мне говорят, что быстрее ветра
Летают доносы.

Я лишь за него боюсь – в чей бы дом он
Ни зашел – кого-нибудь да заденет шуткой.
Злой язык – ядовитый дракон, сторож
Беззащитного сердца.

Что же, раз нравится нам скользить по краю
Жизни, как сатирам – по краю чаши,
Пусть уж тогда звучит она, наливаясь
Не вином – так звоном.

XII

Квинтия, видно, мои письма теперь перестанут
Душу твою бередить – стало опасно писать:
В сплетен горящем кольце – скоро из нашего дома
Разве что мышь ускользнет с тонкой свирелью своей,
Бросит меня в тишину – рыбой на выжженный берег,
Может быть, бросит и Рим…
                              Брошу, наверно, и я,
Если глухие шаги ищущих смерть легионов
Шепот любовный и плач вовремя не заглушат.
Если же нет – и Молва жертвы потребует все же, –
Путь добровольный к теням боги оставили всем.
Жаль, что с собою не взять мне ни колечка, ни книги,
Чаши любимой не взять
                              – той, что мне друг подарил… –
Звонкое имя его спрячу во рту, как монету –
Рядом с другой, что гребцу платою за перевоз.

96

XI

Cynthia – he gave me a bowl yesterday,
With silver satyrs dancing round the edge.
What will I have occasion to drink from it?
Which of us first

Is destined for exile – me for unfaithfulness,
Him for a sarcastic nature and tongue?
Everyone tells me that faster than the wind
Denunciations are flying.

I am only afraid for him – whichever house
He visits – he always offends someone with a joke.
An evil tongue is a poisonous dragon, the guard
Of a defenceless heart.

What of it, maybe we like to slide on the edge
Of life, like the satyrs on the rim of the bowl?
Well then, let it resound when it's pouring out
Not wine, but a peal of bells.

XII

Cynthia, it's clear that now my letters will cease
Irritating your soul – it's too dangerous to write:
In this burning circle of rumours – maybe the mouse
Will steal away soon from our house with its fine reed pipe
And cast me into silence, a fish on to a scorched shore.
Perhaps it will cast aside Rome as well,
                    As I, too, probably will,
If the muffled steps of legions seeking death
Do not stifle the loving cry and whisper first.
If not – and Rumour still needs victims after all –
There's the voluntary way to the shadows the gods have left open to all.
It's a shame that I can't take a ringlet, or a book,
I can't take my beloved bowl –
                        the one he gave me…
His musical name I will hide in my mouth, like a coin –
Near to the other that's to pay the oarsman's fee.

* * *

Низкие тучи, останки сухой травы,
За гнилым забором – клочки ботвы,
Щебень дороги, хромаюшей спьяну вниз, –
Не английский пейзаж, расставленный, как сервиз:
Гулкий дуб, реки фамильное серебро, –
Нет, еловое выломанное ребро
Поперек тропы, обгорелый сруб,
Среди прочих торчащий, как черный зуб,
И такое поле – дождя косая сажень –
Где любой идущий – и даже Господь – мишень.

The low clouds...

The low clouds, the shreds of dry grass,
Beet leaves tufting behind the decayed fence,
The gravel path staggering blind-drunk down:
This is no English landscape, sleek as fine china,
With ancestral oaks and the family silver of a brook:
No: here the snare of a dropped fir branch
Lies across every path, trees hold charred stumps
In their midst like blackened teeth:
And in fields there's no help from the storm-crossed showers
That have it in for everyone, even God.

[CK]

СЕВЕРНАЯ ЭЛЕГИЯ

В разгаре лета коченеет сад,
Сжимают липы камешки бутонов,
Дождь хлещет розу, как маркиз де Сад
Поруганную девственность; антонов,
Максимов, кать не выкрикать из луж,
В ручье под ряской водяная крыса
Знакомая не бьет хвостом; и душ
Ловец – не ловит их: ловил, но скрылся.
Намокший ангел, враз отяжелев,
Сидит в кустах и выжимает тогу,
Прилипшую к коленям; красный лев
Июля мрачно смотрит на дорогу
Сквозь водяные прутья; рыбий глаз
Блестит из скользкой тучи – не затем ли,
Чтобы еще воды подлить. Соблазн
Из чаш цветочных выплеснут на землю.

Так вот он, север, брызжущий на всех
От вечной стирки сморщенной ладонью, –
Здесь может показаться, даже грех
Смывается не кровью, а водою.
Нет, не хитро на юге расцвести,
В Кампанье, в винограднике Прованса, –
Не то, что здесь, зажав себя в горсти,
Где кончились дрова и зонт порвался.
Здесь остается греться изнутри,
Глотать огонь, касаться смуглой кожи,
Взмывая на холмы – гори, гори! –
Скользя в ущелья, вспыхивать: я тоже!
Зажжем-ка лампу. Кружится стена,
Из-за спины твоей кивают вещи,
И плоти полуночная страна
Уже не так темна, не так зловеща.
Да будет свет, упавший на бедро,
Взбираясь вверх, искать соленой влаги
На впалом животе, – вот так перо
Задумчивое бродит по бумаге.

Northern Elegy

At the height of summer the garden freezes,
Lime trees still squeeze their tiny pebble buds,
Rain whips a rose, like the Marquis de Sade
Tortured virginity; you call but the Antons,
Katyas, Maxims won't be called out of puddles,
The same old water rat sits under weed
Now, though, his tail is still; the fisher of souls
Has no souls in his net; he's slunk away to hide.
An angel, soaked through, suddenly cumbersome,
Crouches in the bushes wringing out
The toga stuck to his knees; July looms,
A red lion, glumly watching the road
Through watery branches: there, a fishy eye
Flashes from slippery clouds, more water still
To come? Seduction spills
Down from flowery bowls to the earth below.

This is the North, splashing us all with its
Palms, wrinkled by never-ending laundry,–
Here it shows its face, where even sin
Is washed away by water, not by blood.
To blossom in the South is no big deal,
In Champagne, in the vineyards of Provence,–
Unlike here, where we muster all our strength,
Where the firewood's used up, umbrella torn.
Here we are left to warm up from within,
To swallow fire, and finger swarthy skin,
Climbing up to higher ground – burn, burn! –
Sliding into hollows to ignite: me too!
Let's light the lamp. The walls begin to spin,
And from behind your back things nod their heads,
The midnight land of flesh has changed, and now
It's not so dark and not as ominous.
And this light that's fallen on these hips,
Will push on forth to seek out salty moisture
Across a sunken stomach – as a pen
That's lost in thought, will wander over paper.

Дождь за окном. Двух слитных тел ковчег
Качается, сквозь водяные двери
Вплывая в ночь; как только человек
Уснет – встают недремлющие звери.
И красный лев уже готов напрячь
Все мускулы и рассыпает искры,
Но ты лежишь, прозрачен и горяч, –
Как бы светильник, поднесенный близко, –
И звери растворяются в лучах,
Захлопнув бездны – бархатные пасти. –
Да, это север: если не зачах
От холода – то от огня не спасся.

Косые облака – следы когтей,
На крыше флюгер крылышками вертит.
Что если правда в этой темноте
Стремление к тебе – стремленье к смерти?
Душа скользит в полете за душой –
То вверх, то вниз – дрожащая кривая –
И Бог дневной еще летит со мной,
И Бог ночной из-за плеча кивает.
Так мало солнца, что его всегда
Приходится держать внутри, сгорая.
Течет по крыльям ангела вода,
Под ветром тога хлопает сырая;
Он молча плачет, глядя, как мы спим –
Не просто спим – ночному Богу служим,–
И по дороге стелется, как дым,
Тяжелое крыло влача по лужам.

Outside it's raining; here, two bodies merge
Into an ark that sways, through watery doors
It sails into the night; the moment people
Fall asleep – unsleeping beasts come forth.
Here's the red lion, ready, poised to flex
Every muscle, his body scatters sparks,
While you lie still, translucent and white hot
And glowing, like a light bulb by my face,
And all the beasts dissolve into your rays,
The black holes of their velvet jaws slammed fast.
And that's the North – if you don't waste away
From cold – there's no escaping from the fire.

These wisps of slanting clouds are marks from claws
The blades of a weather vane whizz round.
What if in this darkness the only truth is
That as I reach for you I reach for death?
One soul in flight slides in another's wake
Rising and falling it quakes and twists its way
And for now the God of day flies with me
And the God of night nods me his greeting.
Here the sun's so scarce we have no choice
But to keep it inside while we're burning.
Water's trickling down the angel's wings,
In the wind his sodden toga's flapping,
Silently he cries, watching as we sleep
And as we sleep we serve the God of night –
And so he drifts like smoke along the road,
One heavy wing still trailing through the puddles.

The Soul of Paris

1

What can you see of Paris in five days? What can you grasp of the world if you live to 20, 30, 70? Time is relative: as a baby can prove wiser than an old man, a town can go, like a bullet, straight to the heart, or just graze the edge of consciousness. At high speed your vision loses focus, but gains something which, gliding along unhurriedly, you do not experience: the juxtaposition of plains, a sudden opening up of space.

But this is not really so sudden; from birth where do we turn our souls if not to the West, the very symbol of which is Paris? In this city there is not a single unfamiliar street, square or building – all has been absorbed long ago from books that became a part of us, we adopted so faithfully, experienced, read over and over again to ourselves and aloud, poured over hundreds of times – like the face of a beloved to the fingers of somebody blind. All of us have been coming here since childhood, have wandered for days on end, unseen and with eyes closed; when these are opened at last, that is, when you find yourself here in the flesh, recognition is instantaneous. It is a stunning and sentimental effect, a favourite in Indian films where the orphan who was lost in infancy finally finds, and is reunited with his family in floods of tears and waves of sugary music. That is how it is for a Russian, who is also a foundling, who always suspected deep down that he was a part of the cherished European whole, but was, for some reason, banished so unfairly to the awful snows, to the edge of the world.

If your inner eyes are focussed in one direction for long enough, perhaps your physical gaze will be endowed, one day, with sudden depth? If the eye is already focussed on sharpness, perhaps, even as it flies about and pants for breath, it might catch, with a glance to one side out from under the eyelashes, the hidden duality of the face of Paris, the male-female smile that is faintly discernible in the appearance of Notre Dame and Saint Chapelle. Saint Chapelle flickers on my retina as the feminine beginning of Paris; the masculine, strange as it may seem, emerges as Notre Dame.

This is not only because of the two yellowish, phallic towers, cleaned of the city soot as though of a layer of our sins; although these are partly why. When you climb to the base of those towers, hating and cursing yourself for this tiring concession to the rituals of tourists, you suddenly see, before your very eyes, heavy droplets of stone carving; they are undoubtedly masculine things, and cover the towers right to their very tops. The stone is the colour of skin: there's a strange sensation that the towers are living flesh, increased by the fact that, when you look around, you find yourself surrounded by palpable apostles, angels and saints, which are level with you, near to you, in the same heavens. It's true, there are gargoyles there as well.

You follow their gaze and look down and along – not so much Paris beneath you as its well-proportioned plan, a living map, with blood-vessel roads, the tense but supple line of the spinal cord reaching from the Louvre to the Tuileries, across the glimmering Trocadero to the Champs Élysées and further, beyond the hard Place d'Étoile with its harsh, barbed rays, to the diffuse, unsteady, smoky-glassed building of La Défense. This is the very capacity of the male gaze, grasping not the sensual details, but the schema, the image, the essence: the capacity which opens up from the height of Notre Dame.

From the top of Saint Chapelle you cannot see anything; it is almost entirely hidden by new developments – like blind and grey garments. The church itself is a deep bosom, pulsating with a dim light; when at first you find yourself inside, you feel stifled, awkward that you have glimpsed something your eyes were not meant to see. From within the church is colourful: the walls, columns and ceiling are purple, green and gold. When the Gothic loses its severity it becomes complaisant and tender, drawing eyes towards it. The apse plays with arches, retreating with concave semicircles, splashing out, and then back again, retreating once more; it is folded like a concertina, the edges of the folds are fine, scarlet columns which reveal narrow entrances, dark cracks, dissolving depths. In the round windows along the walls is red and blue stained glass. From a rose window petals stream out, with golden lilies against the blue.

But the real kingdom of stained glass is not here, but on the upper storey, where the green sky of the ceiling blooms with golden stars, and the long windows surge upwards like the pipes of an organ. Their colour – purple and blue – is so piercing it seems to turn into sound. In each window there are dozens of biblical scenes, encircled by the tragic, New Testament girdle – embroidery that is detailed, but divinely inspired, imbued with a light that comes from within, that is not visible, only intuitive. The female gaze on the world is a gaze from within.

Saint Chapelle is depth, concavity, vacillation; the hand stretches to touch the coloured folds of the arches, the gaze strains inwards to the coloured, pulsating gloom. The green leaves of the rose window are, like time, intangible.

Notre Dame is convexity, hardness, the clarity of warm, golden flesh. The triangular wings of the gargoyles, the heavy knobs of carving fill one's palm with space, with the substance of being.

The twin kernel, rent from its stone protection, has a faintly discernible smile, the male-female soul of Paris.

2

The Gothic is love. It tears upwards towards a beloved God, higher and higher, in its tormented effort to catch, achieve, touch – an insatiable and endless effort to bring the earthly word, imprisoned in stone, to Him. Strictly speaking, it has already ceased to be stone, for it has become a flower, a bunch of grapes, a forest thicket, a flood, a small captive angel imprisoned in a carved tower, the white clothes of a saint which have turned into a rose. The world opens up and turns inside out – here am I blooming, growing, sweetly smelling, Your creation, Your love, with towers, fruits, kings and apostles, angels, demons – it gushes upwards, ring after ring, tier after tier, step after step. Here am I, take me, I am Yours! – the world whispers to God, reaching out to Him with the shoots of its towers which narrow to a point in exhaustion.

The Gothic is imbued with Eros. What is crucial is not the masculinity of the vertical, which lies on the surface and draws attention to itself, but the endless variety of forms which stone adopts, moulded by an internal heat; the readiness to abandon its essence and become, for God's eye, whatever necessary – a tree, a beast, a person, the capricious currents of a stream – only notice, touch, discover me, my Beloved! The carving is so unfailing, so generous in giving of itself; the despairing surge upwards is so purposeful; the sacrifice is so unselfish. The Gothic is passion.

Passion, conscious of its hopelessness, and of the tragedy of its earthly existence, is grief-stricken and impulsive, and is the counterpoise to the cool, light joy that pours into a temple of antiquity. Greek porticoes and columns are also filled with love and gratitude towards the harmonious cosmos, but here there is no all-consuming emotion that is concentrated in one direction, burning up from inside – it is dispersed among the pantheon of gods. Even if the temple is dedicated to one god in particular, there will be other divinities, unseen but nearby, which create balance in the world, an organised choir in which a single voice, however strong, is lost. Paganism is a choir, Christianity is a solo.

A choir does not need to move in order to survey space, because it is itself space. A solo is a lonely, wandering point in perpetual motion. The Gothic temple, unlike that of antiquity, is this perpetual motion and, what's more, is directed not only upwards. The tension between the obviously masculine towers and the feminine dark of the portal is huge – however does the stone hold up?

The portal is a widening and narrowing universe of endless rings; around it, near to the corners, are the inclining figures of tsars in thrones, martyrs, saints, heroes, maidens, trembling leaves brimming with the juice of fruit; they disappear into the black point of the gates, and run off again in circles. The cathedral is a cosmos that's only just been created, with obvious remnants of the recent chaos, and the traces of God's fingertips. Cologne cathedral is a good example of this, where chaos has not quite been transformed into a cosmos, as though it cooled and set when only half way there: not a phenomenon, but a process. It is not possible to glimpse the nooks and crannies of this world from just one, two or even three vantage points. The secret is in movement – only slowly circling around in the dark, heavy mass where wonderful features are already emerging, do their appearance, life, and growth become visible. The Gothic is movement; like love, incidentally.

In a sense, the opposite of the Gothic is the Modern, perverted like the elderly babies of Beardsley. The sensuality of the Modern is incredible, but it does not have the readiness of the Gothic to give of itself, to change into anything that its beloved desires; the Modern has the flexibility of an acrobat who is entertaining the public by tying his body into all kinds of knots. The Modern is cold and surrounded by distorting mirrors, in which it glimmers as a shadow that's sometimes Greek, sometimes Roman, and sometimes Gothic. The Modern is sated and voluptuous, while the Gothic is innocent and insatiable. The Modern only plays games, sometimes splendid and light, sometimes weighty and clumsy, sometimes elegant, sometimes awkward; the Gothic thinks only of love and death and, therefore, extremely seriously. In fact, is there any occupation more serious than love?

The Modern is the reflection of a sinful, fallen world which relishes its sin and makes a game out of it. The Gothic is a reflection of the same world – but of its efforts to rise from the ashes. It, too, is incredibly sensual, but quite different. However inventive, however reckless the stone of medieval towers may be in its efforts to lose its stony essence and transform into a supple, pliant stone that's pleasing to God, however sensual its trembling carving may be – all the same, the Gothic contains no sin, for it comprises only fire, and fire is pure.

СОБОРЫ

1

Теряя в сумерки привычную опору,
Затянут небосвод в водоворот собора
И медленно кружится вместе с ним:
Там шелестит крыло, там светит нимб,
Там в каменном раю пывут Адам и Ева,
И где-то на краю, позеленев от гнева,
Трепещет бес, как высохший листок,
Когтями уцепясь за водосток.

Быстрее к центру, медленее к кромке
Вращается отдельная воронка –
Портал – за кругом круг, за рядом ряд –
Земли обетованной виноград,
Апостолы в плащах, властители на тронах,
Герои на конях и ангелы в коронах
Лучей: они плывут на Страшный Суд.
Болтают девы, ангелы поют,
Мерцают мученики, словно в ночь глухую
Светильники; и голуби воркуют.
Но волны башен, черных, как леса,
Взмывают, заглушая голоса.

Cathedrals

1

As the twilight swallows familiar buttresses,
The skies are drawn to the whirlpool of a cathedral,
They slowly revolve, pulled by its undertow:
Here feathers rustle, there gleams a halo,
There's Adam and Eve in a paradise of stone,
And somewhere at the side there sits a demon,
Quivering like a leaf and green from anger,
Grasping at the guttering with its talons.

Faster into the centre, slower outwards
The solitary twister spins around –
A portal – with ring after ring, row after row –
The grapes that hang from the vine of the Promised Land,
Apostles in cloaks and rulers in their thrones,
Heroes on horseback, and angels wearing crowns
Made from rays of light drift on to Doomsday.
Maidens chatter, while angels sing in praise,
Faces of martyrs are flickering, like lamplight
On a gloomy night, and pigeons softly coo.
But the waves of towers, black as a forest,
Rush upwards, their flight muffling all voices.

2

Ты помнишь тот собор, где всадник деревянный
Гарцует, как во сне, в замедленном сияньи,
Не замечая змея под собой,
Поверженного собственной рукой, –
И даже конь его под действием наркоза
Не чувствует когтей, раскрывшихся, как роза,
На животе своем, ни шороха толпы,
И звон колоколов – как звон его копыт.

Ты помнишь шар в огне, подобно колыбели
Свисавший с потолка – пустые параллели,
Меридианы – ленты чугуна
С бутонами свечей? Еще горит одна,
Зажженная тобой, покуда – к небу зоркий,
Но к дольнему слепой, сквозь нас глядел Георгий,
Скача вкруг алтаря, к которому ни тут,
Ни там таких, как мы, не подведут.

2

Remember the cathedral in which a wooden horseman
Prances, as though dreaming, through light in slow motion,
He doesn't see the snake lying on the ground
Slain by one fell stroke of his mighty hand –
Even his charger that's gripped by narcosis
Does not feel the claws which are opening, like roses,
On its stomach, does not hear how the crowd moves,
The ringing of the bells could be his hooves.

Remember the sphere in flames, like a baby's cradle
Suspended from the ceiling – empty parallels,
Meridians – the iron ribbons with
The buds of candles? There is one still lit
Which you set alight; when, seeing the heavens in focus,
But blind to the earthly, St George was gazing through us,
Galloping round the altar, but you and I,
Are not the types to venture up that aisle.

3

Не камень – ливень рушится наверх –
Как будто в пику тем, кого Господь отверг,
Кто падает, кривляясь, вверх пятами
И по карнизам скачет пузырями.
Стена течет, делясь на рукава,
Потоки башен, фразы и слова
Мучительной резьбы, улыбку человечью,
Поскольку нагота воды подобна речи.
Зачем она течет? Чтобы сказать «люблю».
Так птицей притворится – кораблю,
Чтобы скользить вперед, и теплым бризом – блюзу,
Так камню – стать водой, избавиться от груза
И хлынуть к небесам: смотри, любимый Бог,
Возьми меня, я Твой, не камень я – поток,
Я гибок, как лоза – приняв любую позу –
То дерево, то зверь, то каменная роза,
Стремясь к Тебе наверх, я буду всем подряд,
Чтоб только твой остановился взгляд.
Вода шумит листвой, пустив ростки витые,
Где спят вороны, ангелы, святые,
Висит органа певчее гнездо.
Струится камень, сдерживая вздох,
Как слезы, как гроза под грохот колокольный,
Но там, на высоте, где Бог коснется (больно!) –
Там вдруг преображается вода
В огонь палящий, в молнию креста.

3

Not stone – but rain is collapsing upwards,
As though to spite those God has turned away,
Who twist and turn in their fall, heels skyward,
And, like bubbles, bounce from ledge to ledge.
These walls are flowing; they divide into streams,
Into floods of towers, and the phrases and words
Of torturous carving, and into a human smile,
For the nakedness of water resembles speech.
Why does it flow? So it can say 'I love you'.
As a ship mimics bird flight to slide ahead
And the blues takes on the guise of a warm breeze,
So stone becomes water and shrugs off its weight,
Gushes to the skies; look, beloved God!
Take me, I'm yours, no stone am I, but a flood,
Supple as a vine, I can take any pose:
Now a tree, now a beast, now a rose made of stone,
Reaching for you above, I'm everywhere in turn
As I try these many ways to arrest your gaze.
The water sounds like leaves, with its curling shoots
In which ravens sleep, and angels, and the saints,
The singing nest of the organ hangs in the air.
This stone is flowing, it suppresses a sigh,
Like tears, like a storm that breaks to the thunder of bells,
But there, at the top, where God touches (it hurts!) –
There, suddenly, water is transformed
Into a scorching flame, a lightning cross.

4

Мерцает у вокзала не звезда –
Галактика собора, всем чужда.
Вращается многоугольный хаос,
На мелочный порядок натыкаясь
Гостиниц, булочных, бетонных коробков,
Приличных улочек и овощных лотков.
Здесь разбомбили все – так чисто вымел веник,
Что ни один кирпич – не современник
Остроконечных трубчатых костей,
По шляпку в небо вогнанных гвоздей,
Чье кружево покрыто черной сажей. –
Конечно, то грехи и мысли наши,
Витавшие вокруг из века в век.
Плывет собора дымчатый ковчег,
И в нем снует толпы цветная рыба,
Поскольку эта стрельчатая глыба
Пуста. Между колонной и стеной
Войдешь и встанешь – будешь новый Ной.

4

That's not a star, glimmering by the station,
But the galaxy of a cathedral, foreign to all;
Its polygonal chaos is spinning around
And stumbling against the detail of street plans:
The hotels and bakers, and concrete boxes,
Respectable side streets and vegetable kiosks.
Here everything was bombed – swept away so clean
That not a single brick is a contemporary
Of those sharp-pointed, tubular bones
Those nails hammered into the heavens,
Whose lace is coated in black soot
Which is, of course, our sins and our thoughts
That have hovered here age after age.
The cathedral, a smoke-coloured ark, will sail,
Inside a crowd, a coloured fish, darts round,
Because this lump, crowned with a vaulted ceiling
Is empty. Between a column and a wall
You enter and rise up – you will be a new Noah.

* * *

Ангел с лютнею в руках
Над Европой не кружится,
А прекрасных шпилей прах
И сухая черепица –

Точно пыльные смычки,
Скрипок сломанные грифы:
Волны музыки, легки,
Высохли, оставив рифы

Стен, песок туристских толп,
Не опасных ни на йоту.
Музыка – кипящий столб
Водяной, и запах йода,

Грубый свет соленых звезд,
И крушенье, и кощунство, –
Высохла. Лишь певчий дрозд
Совершенствует искусство

На карнизе, меж камней,
В золотой воздушной сфере,
И в соборе холодней,
Чем в груди у Люцифера.

Лишь дрожащие сады
Ждут горячих губ Франциска,
Воин, бронзовой воды
Зачерпнув, склонился низко,

Но не пьет, блюдя устав
Статуй. В урне спят отбросы.
Шмель гудит, как Минотавр,
В гулком лабиринте розы.

Circling over Europe...

Circling over Europe
There's no angel with a lute,
But the dust of splendid spires
And dry pantiles –

Like cobweb-covered bows,
And broken violin scrolls:
Waves of music, light as air
Have dried out, leaving walls

As reefs, sandy throngs
Of tourists, that pose no danger.
Music – a seething column
Of water, and iodine odour,

And garish salty starlight,
And ruin, and blasphemy, –
Has dried out. Only the song thrush
Reaches art's epiphany

On a cornice, amongst stones
In the golden sphere of the air,
While in the church it's colder
Than the bosom of Lucifer.

Only trembling gardens await
St Francis' burning lips,
A warrior scoops bronze water,
Bends down lower, but doesn't drink –

Obeying the rules for statues.
In an urn rubbish dozes
A bee hums, like a minotaur,
In the echoing maze of roses.

* * *

Я хочу в Венецию – как лицом в траву,
Посмотреть, как выглядит душа моя наяву.
От нее закат, как камин, отгорожен цветным экраном,
И часы расцвели на стебле четырехгранном:
Стрелок тычинки; горьковатого звона завязь
Никогда не созреет, подставленных губ касаясь.
Там копье проросло, как в озере остролист,
И герой, словно рыба, выловлен: запеклись
Бронзовые чешуйки – он умер сразу.
И дома поставлены в воду, как в зеленую вазу.
Под ногой ступень качается, как листок,
И пролеты мостов прерывисты, словно вздох,
Словно в горле речь – не находя участья,
Медлит – начаться ей или не начаться.
Есть у счастья свои приметы и у несчастья тоже:
Покрывается камень гусиной кожей,
А спина волны каменеет; на водосточной трубе
Выступает испарина, как на губе.
То ли в любви, то ли в битве –

                                сжав друг друга руками,
Смертной дрожью объяты оба – вода и камень.

I want to go to Venice...

I want to go to Venice – like pressing my face
Into grass – to see my soul as it is awake.
With a bright fire-guard, the sunset is shielded from my soul,
And a clock has blossomed on a tetrahedral stem:
The hand of the stamen; the ovary of bitter chimes
Will never ripen, while they touch the lips proffered to them.
A spear sprouted upwards, like holly in a lake,
And the hero was caught, like a fish: his bronze scales
Dried out into a crust – and he died at once.
The houses are stood in water like in a green vase.
Underfoot a step gives way like a leaf,
And the sweeping spans of the bridges are broken, like breath,
Like speech in a throat – when it finds no sympathy,
And slows down – should it begin or not begin?
Happiness has its signs as unhappiness does:
A stone breaks into goose pimples all over,
The back of a wave stiffens; on a drainpipe
Perspiration prickles, as it might on a lip.
In love, or maybe war –
                                        clasping each other,
Both convulsed by trembling – are stone and water.

* * *

Скрещены кости проспектов – белым-белы,
Ветром обглоданы, бешеным, словно волк,
Серые крыши – зубья тупой пилы –
В сердце врезаются. Выпьем – а будет толк

Или не будет, сможет ли алкоголь
Перенести через огненную реку,
Став ковром-самолетом, – и через боль,
Скорость развив, – сказать тебе не могу.

Быстро откупорив тайную дверь, – глоток
Выпьем, пока не заметила нас сама
Старая ведьма, мотающая клубок
Пухлого снега в темном углу, – зима.

The bones of avenues lie crossed...

The bones of avenues lie crossed – bright white,
Gnawed clean by a wind that's wild as a wolf,
Grey roofs are the teeth of a blunted saw
That cuts into the heart. We'll have a drink

But will it help or not, can the alcohol pass
Over this river of fire, and become
A magic carpet: gathering speed, can it move
Beyond this pain? I cannot say.

Pop the secret door quickly, and we'll drink
A gulp, before we are noticed by
The old witch who's busy rolling a ball
Of puffy snow, in a dark corner – winter.

* * *

Снег – сам себе источник света.
Он – прошлая листва, рассыпчатое лето,
В нем водяные замерли уста,
И, как в гробу хрустальном, все цвета
Ревниво заперты, но целы.
Снег не разделит нас, он – продолженье тела,
Движенья, призрачная цель
Творенья. Роза белая – метель,
Смотри, колышется над нами,
И ветер – червь – впивается в нее,
Рвет сердце ей… – Возьми ее руками,
Вдохни ее густое забытье.
Смотри, как лепестки ее упруги,
Шипы воздушны и остры,
Обнимешь – через сомкнутые руки
Со стоном продираются миры.
Снег – продолженье тел – из ледяной коры
Своей – самоубийственный прорыв
К игре частиц, снег – продолженье звука –
Сквозь фугу – вверх – до тишины…
Ты не пришел сегодня – что ж, не нужно:
Став тенью снежной, плотью вьюжной,
Касанья губ – особенно нежны.

Snow is the source of its own light...

Snow is the source of its own light.
It is last year's leaves and the crumbling summer,
Watery mouths within it have frozen still,
And, as though in a crystal grave, all the colours
Are jealously closed, but intact and whole.
Snow doesn't divide – it extends our bodies,
Our movements, this is the phantom aim
Of creation. A white rose is a blizzard,
See how it's heaving above our heads,
While the wind – a worm – is feeding inside it,
Tearing out the heart... Pick it up,
Take a deep breath of its thick oblivion.
Look how its petals are taut,
Its thorns are airy and sharp,
You clasp them, yet worlds still force their way,
With a groan, through a closed hand.
Snow extends bodies – through its icy crust
There's a suicidal break into what
Is a game of particles; snow extends sound
Through a fugue, and upwards to peacefulness...
You didn't come today – so what? You did not have to.
Now, the shadow of snow and the flesh of a blizzard
Are the touch of lips, and seem especially tender.

* * *

Дождь выпивает зиму, как вампир,
Порвав ее тугие кружева
И подточив рассудочный ампир
Ее колонн, дойдя до естества

Глухих дорог и ледяных канав,
Он пьет их тело чистое – и лед,
Вцепляясь в корни прошлогодних трав,
Покорно тает, превращаясь в мед.

И тает воздух – складками рубах
Вокруг деревьев, превращаясь в дым,
И тает время на твоих губах,
Как только прикасаются к моим.

Like a vampire...

Like a vampire, rain drinks from winter
Through the holes it's torn in her fine white lace,
It has eaten away at her rational Empire
Columns, and reaches the very essence

Of forgotten roads and icy ditches,
It drinks their pure bodies; and the ice,
Seizing on the roots of last year's grasses
Obediently melts, turns honey-like,

And the air melts, like the folds of a slip
Wrapped around tree trunks, it turns into smoke,
And time will melt upon your lips
The moment they meet with mine and touch.

* * *

Ты – мое небо, слоистый дымок горизонта,
Тот, за которым без слов исчезает Изольда,
Счеты покончив с сюжетом – с каленым железом,
С гроздью лучей, истекающих соком над лесом,
Где она дремлет с Тристаном, и меч между ними
Светится тускло. Пейзаж превращается в зимний,
Снег засыпает тела, утомленное солнце
Прячется в стеганой туче. Но меч остается.
В нем-то загвоздка: пока меж тобою и мною
Твердо блестит он – замерзшей речной полосою
(Так между буквой и речью твердеет бумага), –
Мне не исчезнуть, не сделать последнего шага.

You're my sky...

You're my sky, layered streaks of cloud on the horizon,
Past them, without words, Isolde disappears,
Scores are settled with the plot – with molten metal,
With branching rays that pour juice-like over the forest
Where she slumbers with Tristan, and between them the sword
Dimly gleams. The landscape transforms into winter,
Snow covers their bodies, the wearied sun
Hides in a quilted cloud. But the sword is still there.
And there's the rub – while between you and I
It coldly shines, like the flash of a frozen stream
(Like paper hardens between the letter and speech) –
I can't disappear, I can't make the final leap.

* * *

Снег стареет, как с детства знакомый актер,
Провисает, как занавес, так что не видно походки
В мутном зеркале ветра – и весел ты, жив или мертв –
Не имеет значенья, румян или бледен, – гример,
Подлетая, по скулам проводит пуховкой.

И становишься вдруг никому не знаком.
Ты один в этот вечер – любое движение, значит,
Растворяется тут же, отражаясь ни в ком,
Снег валится за раму, и тьма подзывает кивком,
И идешь, и ложишься у края, свернувшись в калачик.

Кто лишен отраженья в другом, тот лишен бытия,
Глух, и нем, и безвиден. Качаются гнезда вороньи.
Колесо пронеслось – серебрится в рубцах колея,
Небеса разорвались – дымятся края,
И луна проплывает в огромной морозной короне.

Snow grows old...

Snow grows old, like an actor you knew as a child,
It sags like a drape, so that footsteps keep on escaping
The dim mirror of the wind – you're happy, alive or dead –
It's not important, flushed or pale, – here's a make-up artist,
Surging upwards, tracing cheekbones with a powder puff.

Suddenly you're somebody that nobody knows.
Alone on this evening, your every movement will
Dissolve in an instant, without reflection,
Snow falls outside the frame, dark beckons with a nod,
And you lie, curled up, along the edge of the bed.

Without a reflection in somebody, you are without being.
Deaf, and mute, and unseen. Crows' nests are swaying.
The wheel has rolled past, its tracks are silvery scars,
The heavens have torn apart – their edges billowing,
And the moon drifts past in a wide, frozen halo.

* * *

Фасад в зеленой паутине:
Сияют окна, вытек мозг.
И день святого Валентина,
Безумный, выкатил на мост.

Пойдем куда-нибудь сквозь стужу, –
Не сразу же в подземный ад!
Повсюду с грацией верблюжьей
Двугорбые сугробы спят.

И на углах замерзли девки,
А на лотках – хурма, айва,
И город выставлен на древке
Невы, как вражья голова.

Сильней дыхание от ветра
Раскачивается внутри –
И сердце на незримой ветке
Багровым яблоком горит.

И солнце – ноющая ранка,
И церковь – облака двойник,
И мертвый снег, как падший ангел,
К забору крыльями приник.

A façade is caught...

A façade is caught in a web of green,
The windows glint, but the brain's leaked away.
Out rushed the day of St Valentine,
A madman, and over the bridge he sailed.

Let's go out for a walk through the cold
And not descend yet to hell underground
All around us with a camel-like grace
Lie two-humped drifts of snow, sleeping sound.

And girls are freezing on the street corners,
While stalls sell persimmons and quinces,
The city is mounted high on the stake
Of the Neva, a trophy, the enemy's head.

It's the wind that makes the breath that you draw
Surge inside you with such violent force,
And your heart, aloft on a unseen bough
Hangs like a scarlet apple, and glows.

And the sun is a festering sore,
And the church is the doppelgänger of a cloud,
And the dead snow, like a fallen angel
Has pressed its wings up to the railings.

ОТТЕПЕЛЬ

Под соснами протаяли круги,
Как от бессоницы.
Пустых берез шатаются верхи –
Сырые звонницы,

Лишенные давно колоколов
Зеленых, лиственных,
И ветер, как топор, поверх голов
Насвистывает.

И свет истлел – и обтянул поля,
Как кости черепа.
Кащея, сребролюбца, февраля
Казна исчерпана.

Мерцает костью пожелтевший лед
Под вербой-свечкою,
Пока ворона мертвый снег клюет,
Седая, вещая.

Thaw

Circles have thawed beneath pine trees, as though
Around tired eyes.
The tops of empty birches sway –
Damp bell towers

Bereft long ago of their green and
Deciduous bells –
And overhead the wind, like an axe,
Whistles.

And light has decayed, and fits over fields
Like cranial bones.
February has turned scrooge at last, worn and
Money-grubbing.

Yellowed ice glimmers like bone beneath
A pussy willow candle,
While a crow pecks away at dead snow,
Grey, prophesying.

* * *

Снег отступил, как море, обнажив
Тельца травинок мертвых, скорлупу
Сараев, рощ сырые миражи,
На станции – набухшую крупу

Народа в ожиданьи поездов,
Все медлящих отправиться туда,
Куда несется запоздалый вздох
Густого дыма, черного куста.

Торчат стволы, как ржавые ножи,
У рынка в кучу свалены кули.
Снег разомкнул объятья, обнажив
Всю тьму, всю неприкаянность земли.

The snow has receded...

The snow has receded, like a sea, and uncovered
The skeletons of dead grass, the shells
Of barns, damp mirages of groves,
At the station sodden sheaves

Of people stand waiting for trains,
Ever delayed in their departure
To follow the sigh of thick smoke still
Lingering, the trail of black bushes.

Tree trunks stick up, like rusty knives,
Sacks are piled in a heap at the market.
The snow has undone embraces, uncovered
All the darkness, all the restlessness of the earth.

* * *

Мне холодно, мой друг. Весна глядит зимой.
Хвостатая звезда стоит над головой,
И носится кругами ветер бесноватый,
Кусая плащ ночной, где вытерт колкий ворс,
И белыми стежками, вкривь и вкось,
Приляпано окно пылающей заплатой.

Мне холодно. Сосна на глиняной ноге
Качается, зажав ворону в кулаке.
По скользкому крыльцу мужик скребет лопатой.
На стеблях фонарей – погашены цветы,
И судорогой сведены мосты,
И волны, как рукав тюремный, полосатый.

Мне холодно. Висит комета надо мной,
Склонясь, как райский плод на ветке ледяной,
Не нужная земле, еще летящей рядом,
Неся свои сады. Влача соленый шлейф,
И я вот так уйду во тьму; не пожалев,
Наверное, и ты меня проводишь взглядом.

I am cold, my friend...

I am cold, my friend. Spring looks like winter.
There's a long-tailed star in the sky overhead,
The wind is wheeling around like a madcap,
Biting night's mantle that's threadbare and frayed,
On to which clumsy and crooked white stitches
Have tacked a window, like a flaming patch.

I am cold. A pine on its earthen leg
Rocks with a raven clasped in its fist.
A workman's shovel rasps against the roof.
On streetlight stems the flowers are extinguished,
With a spasm the ends of the bridge realign,
Like prison sleeves, the waves are striped.

I am cold. A comet hangs above me,
A fruit of paradise bending an icy branch,
It's no use to the Earth, still flying nearby
With its gardens. Trailing salty streamers,
I, too, vanish into the dark; unperturbed,
I surmise, you follow me with your gaze.

ВЕСНА

Чугунный врач с сиреневым отливом
Обходит вечер шагом кропотливым,
Блестит заколкой в фетровой траве
И шар серебряный несет на голове,
Где плавают изогнутые стены
И червячки засушенных растений,
Автобус трескается, точно яйцо,
Цветные волны бороздят лицо,
Ложатся на бок летаргические церкви
И облака нависший эркер
Вот-вот обвалится.
                    На дне
Непрочной сферы, словно луч в вине,–
Крутящиеся тающие льдинки;
А в центре, не дробясь на дольки, половинки,
Из воска слепленные, ветра и стекла
Горят любовников прозрачные тела.

Spring

A cast-iron rook that's tinged with lilac
Edges round the evening with careful steps,
Shining in the felt grass like a hair-clip
It wears a silver ball upon its head
Wherein distorted walls merge with each other
And withered, dried-out plants kaleidoscope,
A bus cracks into two just as an egg might
And coloured waves trace lines across a face,
Lethargic churches lie down horizontal,
Like a bay window an overhanging cloud
Will crash down any moment now.
                                    In the base
Of the fragile sphere, like light that shines through wine,
Some ice-cubes move in circles as they melt,
While at the centre, not splitting into segments
Moulded out of wax and wind and glass
The translucent bodies of two lovers glow.

ЭЛЕГИЯ НА СМЕРТЬ ЗВЕЗДЫ

Ничего мне не надо. Пусть умирает звезда,
Не исполнив жалких моих, никому не нужных,
Безобразных желаний, стыдящихся на уста
Приходить. Ее смерть прекрасна и ненатужна,
Не замутнена тяжелым моим «хочу», –
Пусть она умирает, припав к твоему плечу
Головою пылающею, недужной.
Для того и развесил август свои сады
В остывающем небе, над дряхлеющею травою,
Чтоб приманивать глупое сердце на смерть звезды, –
Не поймаюсь, не бойся, Господь с тобою,
Не пожелаю лишнего. Вообще
Не пожелаю – то ли жидкость иссякла в жилах,
То ли слишком уж много звезд вотще
Головы серебряные сложило,
Обещанья не выполнив. Хоть одна
Будет избавлена от позора
И умрет свободной, чтобы, достигнув дна,
Тихо лечь – непроглоченная блесна –
Среди битых бутылок и жестяного сора,
Не желание вызывая, но зависть. Ведь это ложь –
Что с пустыми руками ныряют в бездну:
Все оставишь на этом свете, а смерть возьмешь,
Как кольцо, которое слишком тесно,
Чтобы снять его, отправляясь в путь, –
И во тьме летит небесное это тельце,
Заключив в округлом сияньи суть
Своего рассыпавшегося владельца.

Elegy on the Death of a Star

I don't need anything now. Let the star die
Without fulfilling my pitiful wishes that are
Good for nothing, scandalous, and too embarrassed
To come to my lips. Its death is beautiful, unforced,
Not tainted with my weighty demanding 'I want' –
Let it die leant against your shoulder
With its blazing head aching and unwell.
That's the reason August has hung out its gardens
In the cooling sky, above grasses going to seed,
It's to lure a foolish heart to the death of a star –
I won't be caught, don't worry, my dear,
I won't wish for anything too much. In fact I won't
Wish ever again – either my veins have run dry
Or too many stars have laid down
Their silvery lives in vain,
Without fulfilling promises. At least one
Will be spared the shame
And will die at liberty, so when it reaches the bottom
It will lie down quietly – like a spoon-bait unswallowed –
Amongst the broken bottles and tin cans,
And arouse not desire, but envy. For it's a lie
That you dive into the abyss with empty hands:
You leave behind everything except for death
Which you keep like a ring too tight on your finger
To take off, when you set out on your way, –
And as this heavenly body flies through the darkness,
It confines to its round luminescence the essence
Its owner's ashes, now scattered, once contained.

In the Grip of Strange Thoughts
Russian Poetry in a New Era
Edited by J. KATES *with a foreword by* MIKHAIL AIZENBERG

Russian's political revolution of 1990 set off a cultural earthquake of unprecedented impact. But there were tremors four years before. The whole country saw the cracks starting to appear which eventually resulted in the overthrow of the old system, and the collapse of the confining roofs of direction and repression.

This anthology shows how a new generation of Russian poets have responded first to that evolving cultural shift and then to the difficult freedoms of a new era. No longer constrained by bureaucracy or ideology, these writers are producing a new literature of great energy and diversity. Working in styles ranging from traditional to avant-garde to postmodern, they depict the cascading changes in Russian life and culture – through the most intimate details of private lives to the larger images of a nation forging a new path for itself.

BILINGUAL RUSSIAN-ENGLISH EDITION
234 x 156mm   464 pages   1 85224 478 X   £12.95 paper

EVGENY REIN
Selected Poems
Edited by VALENTINA POLUKHINA   *Foreword by* JOSEPH BRODSKY
Translated by ROBERT REID, DANIEL WEISSBORT
& CAROL RUMENS / YURI DROBYSHEV

Evgeny Rein is Russia's greatest living poet. Born in 1935, he belongs to that tragic generation of Russian poets who for decades went unpublished in the Soviet Union, and didn't publish his first book of poems until he was 49. One of Akhmatova's 'magic choir' of young Leningrad poets, he was Joseph Brodsky's mentor and lifetime friend. Brodsky figures in many of his poems, and Brodsky's essay on Rein introduces this selection:

'Rein is unquestionably an elegiac poet. His main theme is the end of things, the end, to put it more broadly, of a world order that is dear – or at least acceptable – to him. The incarnation of

this order in his poetry is the city in which he grew up, the city of Leningrad...Rein not only radically extended the poetic vocabulary and sound palette of Russian poetry; he also broadened and shook up the psychological sweep of Russian lyrics. He is an elegist, but of a tragic stripe. Few among his compatriots would dispute the depth of the despair and exhaustion that darkens these poems...'
– JOSEPH BRODSKY

Poetry Book Society Recommended Translation
BILINGUAL RUSSIAN-ENGLISH EDITION
216 x 138mm   176 pages   1 85224 523 9   £9.95 paper

TATIANA SHCHERBINA
Life Without
Selected Poetry & Prose 1992-2003
Translated and introduced by SASHA DUGDALE

Tatiana Shcherbina has been described as 'one of the most significant figures in contemporary Russian poetry' (*Kommersant'*). In her recent work the elegant and ironic narrator meditates on love, disappointment and loss against the backdrop of Russia's social collapse. Sometimes her poems take the form of overtly political statements ('Dictatorship, democracy'), sometimes new capitalist Russia is reflected merely in the emotional plane – in a poem on lost love she claims she has paid the highest rate: cash.

Whilst her themes are timeless, Shcherbina's settings are distinctly contemporary. She writes about sitting at a computer gazing into the Microsoft Windows; her poems are full of supermarkets, printing cartridges, TV, the environment; she considers applying make-up, drinking alone, falling asleep to the sounds of films in the next room. She has even been criticised for a supposedly anti-Russian stance, yet she understands absolutely what is happening in Russia and is in no way an outsider. Her stance is that of a woman challenging Russia's patriarchal and chauvinist society. However, her poetry is not primarily political, but literary, and she shows great versatility in different forms and genres. Her playfully meditative essays form the perfect counterpoint to her sophisticated and self-aware poetry.

BILINGUAL RUSSIAN-ENGLISH EDITION
216 x 138mm   144 pages   1 85224 642 1   £8.95 paper

ELENA SHVARTS
'Paradise': Selected Poems

Translated and introduced by MICHAEL MOLNAR
with additional translations by CATRIONA KELLY

'Elena Shvarts is a miracle, believe me. Her poetry is the purest of creations' – BELLA AKHMADULINA

'This is an explosive book by a dark, free, northern spirit, a woman born in Leningrad in 1948 but not openly published there until 1989. Bulgakov and Tsvetayeva (and Angela Carter) would feel at home in her violently imagined townscapes and landscapes. 'Paradise' was Peter the Great's word for his newly established city, but in Shvarts' poems the place is everything from a 'glorious dump' to a 'Rosa mystica', a 'gulf of chiming bells' to a sky of crows like 'scraps of burnt archives':

> *A tram swooped up, flushed crimson,*
> *and quietly swallowed me, like a wafer.*

Jagged feeling irradiates the extraordinary *Elegy on an X-ray Photo of My Skull*, but she is capable also of an offbeat narrative pathos, as in *A Parrot at Sea*, where the shipwrecked bird talks and squawks on a plank – and we can read as much as we like into that – as long as it can, before the ocean claims it' – EDWIN MORGAN, *PBS Bulletin*

Each new generation has to reinterpret St Petersburg, the place, the culture and its significance for Russia. Shvarts' haunted and demonic city is nearer Dostoyevsky's than Akhmatova's or Brodsky's. Her poetry draws backwoods, Russian folklore with its cruelty, its religiosity and its quaint humour, into stone, cosmopolitan Petropolis. She brings out both the truth and the irony of Peter the Great's 'Paradise', celebrating and reviling her native city as a crossroads of dimensions, a reality riddled with mythical monuments and religious symbols.

Poetry Book Society Recommended Translation
BILINGUAL RUSSIAN-ENGLISH EDITION
216 x 138mm   160 pages   1 85224 249 3   £8.95 paper